Praise

APERT

Findings from a Rural Life

MARY B. KURTZ

"'It's possible,' said William Blake, 'To see a World in a Grain of Sand / And a Heaven in a Wild Flower.' In this beautiful collection of essays, Mary Kurtz proves Blake right. The lenses provided by her forty years on a ranch in northwestern Colorado—in sight of the Rockies and not far from the Elk River—allow her to write of local life in a universal way, a way that opens into the world of our senses and the world of mystery. No matter where or how you live, these deeply lived and well-told stories will illumine your life. Or so it has been for me."

—PARKER J. PALMER, author of *On the Brink of Everything, Let Your Life Speak, A Hidden Wholeness,* and *The Courage to Teach*

"French philosopher Nicolas Malebranche wrote, 'Attention is the natural prayer of the soul.' If this is true, then Mary Kurtz is a woman who lives her life in prayer, lavishing attention on the land she's rooted to: the Elk River Valley in the alpine altitudes of northern Colorado, where her family ranch lies. With *Apertures: Findings from a Rural Life,* she joins the great tradition of Western American literature, conveying the beauty of the land on a scale both vast and intimate. She gives us both the close-ups and the big picture in her crystalline, contemplative essays."

—JENNY SHANK, author of *Mixed Company,* Colorado Book Award Winner

"These exquisite essays centered on the author and her husband's ranch in the Rocky Mountain foothills illuminate a rural American place, its river and cottonwoods, its elk and cougar, its heavy snows and morning light. The lives of the people, too—their work of feeding and fencing, their love of an old horse, their faithful dogs, a mother's death—are told with grace and insight. The quiet attention brought to this place and these lives make *Apertures* a deeply satisfying read."

—**PRISCILLA LONG**, author of *Fire and Stone: Where Do We Come From? What Are We? Where Are We Going?*

"Mary Kurtz's memoir-in-essays, *Apertures: Findings from a Rural Life*, is the quiet revery of a ranch woman who has lived and worked the land alongside her husband for forty years in the Elk River Valley. Under the gentle and wise ministry of Kurtz, this dark and light landscape of cattle and fireweed, of heartwood and wooly bears, of deep winter freezes and spring lupine ascends into a beautiful backdrop for her spiritual quest and awakening. Kurtz's contemplation of life and mortality in 'each holy place' of this valley, through seasonal and family ritual, places *Apertures* alongside the finest of Western writing."

—**KATHRYN WINOGRAD**, author of *Slow Arrow: Unearthing the Frail Children*

"Mary Kurtz's graceful, pliant sentences leave a charming imprint on the Western landscape. After finishing this book, I went back to the beginning for another round, pausing this time to re-read her most eloquent passages, stunned anew by their grace and beauty."

—**DAVID HICKS**, author of *White Plains*, 2018 Colorado Book Award Finalist, Director of the Maslow Family Graduate Program in Creative Writing, Wilkes University

"Loyalty to place, once a given, is increasingly rare. This deeply felt tribute to a classic western landscape reminds us of its power to enrich our lives."

—**WILLIAM DEBUYS**, author of *The Trail to Kanjiroba: Rediscovering Earth in an Age of Loss*

"Mary B. Kurtz astounds and delights in this meditative collection of personal essays, reflecting, refracting, and luxuriating in the richness of a decidedly rural life. Kurtz wanders through family, community, the natural world—not outside of human dwelling but woven intimately around and to it—and the connection between selfhood and landscape, never pushing toward a specific destination but allowing the reader, always, to enjoy the ride."

—**MEREDITH GRACE THOMPSON**, editor of *BlueHouse Journal*, co-editor of orangeapplepress

APERTURES

APERTURES

findings from a rural life

MARY B. KURTZ

SHANTI ARTS PUBLISHING
BRUNSWICK, MAINE

Apertures: Findings from a Rural Life

Copyright © 2022 Mary B. Kurtz

Published by Shanti Arts Publishing

Cover and interior design by Shanti Arts Designs
Cover image by Christian Sogaard on unsplash.com

Interior images: Illustration at start of each chapter by MaxNadya / 1308247773 on istockphoto.com; pp. 14–15, serena koi on pexels.com; pp. 46–47, pixabay.com; pp. 80–81, valentine kulik on pexels.com; pp. 102–03, meredith fontana on unsplash.com; pp. 118–19, Jeffrey Beall, Tennessee Creek, Colorado, Wikimedia Commons (CC BY 3.0)

"A Crooked and Gnarly Wood" first appeared in *Amsterdam Quarterly* as "A Dark and Gnarled Wood"; "A Rustling in the Oaks" first appeared in *Braided Way: Faces and Voices of Spiritual Practice Perspectives*; "Dendrites and Stars" first appeared in *BlueHouse Journal*.

Scripture taken from the New King James Version®. Copyright © 1982 by Thomas Nelson. Used by permission. All rights reserved.

Shanti Arts LLC
Brunswick, Maine
www.shantiarts.com

Printed in the United States of America

This book is a memoir, written from the author's recollections of experiences that occurred over many years. The dialogue presented in this book is not intended to represent word-for-word transcripts; events and scenes are not precise representations. The names and characteristics of some individuals have been changed to protect privacy. In all cases, the author has remained true to the feeling and meaning of what happened and what was said.

ISBN: 978-1-956056-56-3 (softcover)
ISBN: 978-1-956056-57-0 (ebook)

Library of Congress Control Number: 2022944461

*With deep appreciation and gratitude
for the gift of place.*

CONTENTS

ACKNOWLEDGMENTS

Often, too, our own light goes out, and is rekindled by some experience we go through with a fellow man. Thus we have each of us cause to think with deep gratitude of those who have lighted the flames within us.[1]

—Albert Schweitzer

In my mind, the creative process is circular, finding its way to completion only when it is heard, read, or viewed. When I'm immersed in the journey along that arc, I find myself, at times, questioning the validity and value of my work. And in those moments, a need arises for an outside source of light to make the way clear. It is here that I wish to give thanks to those who have illuminated my path. Without them, this manuscript would not have completed its creative circle.

First, with gratitude to David Hicks for accepting me at sixty-five into the Regis Mile High Low-Residency MFA program. Secondly, I offer thanks to each faculty member with whom I've worked, either in workshop or as a faculty mentor: Sophfronia Scott, David Lazar, TaraShea Nesbitt, Chip Livingston, Jenny Shank, Kristen Iversen, and Kathy Winograd. I particularly wish to acknowledge my thesis advisor, Kathy Winograd, whose early enthusiasm for my writing lifted my spirit to another level of faith and confidence in my work; and to Jenny Shank, my thesis reader, whom I admired for her expertise and master teaching during my third residency.

Lastly, I extend a thanks to the members of my cohort and fellow workshop writers. I am touched each residency by the heartfelt feedback and encouragement I receive. I am incapable of knowing what it is my writing truly communicates without each one of you. With special thanks to Anita Jepson-Gilbert, Ginny Short, Nate Matlock, and Melanie Merle.

PREFACE

No genuine book has a first page. Like the rustling of a forest, it is begotten, God knows where, and it grows, and it rolls, arousing the dense wilds of the forest until suddenly it begins to speak with all the treetops at once.[2]

—Boris Pasternak

HAVE CONCLUDED THAT THIS MAY BE PARTICULARLY TRUE in the case of a collection of essays, for each one possesses its very own beginning. But is there a way to attest to the nascence, the genesis of this book? Is there a point of departure I might identify?

Perhaps, it first begins here.

At home where evergreen and aspen huddle and shade
and arctic willows break the blow of rowdy winds,
I sit and rock in the evenings believing in the order of things.
Like the woods after a rain in the middle of a deadly drought,
scented with moist bark, sated grass and a replenished earth.
It is here my husband says to me,
"You should see the light, the crimson,
the salmon, the beginning of the night."

Now in my mid-sixties, I stand on what Parker J. Palmer, founder of the Center for Courage and Renewal, describes as the "brink of everything."[3] It's from this horizon I wrote to remember, and I wrote in search of what might lie ahead. In the exercise, our agricultural life offered a rich marrow from which to amplify my inner experience. As if I were looking through the aperture of a microscope with its light-gathering qualities, I used a small lens with which to magnify an evocation of my daily life: the rhythms of ranch life, the murmurings of a natural world, and the vagaries and mysteries of aging and mortality. In the writing, I share that intimate intersection between my conscious life and place, the space of transition between sentient awareness and a sense of mystery.

Apertures, a collection of twenty-eight lyric essays, is best defined by its nonlinear structure: a memoir inspired by memory folded into the present followed by ruminations on what lies ahead. Beth Kephart, in her essay, "Honoring the Seams: The Memoir-in-Pieces,"[4] writes, "We are what we remember plus the current circumstance." Martin Heidegger has suggested, too, that time is defined by an awareness of "having been," giving way for the past to exist in the present.[5] So too, concern for potential possibilities related to one's purpose allows for the future to also exist in the present.

As I wrote and revised over a period of ten years, my sense of time as a writer was fluid, shifting from past and present and back again as though traveling along a mobius ribbon, time moving forward yet turning back on itself. Drawing up memories occurred at the same time I witnessed the death of my mother and another decade of my own personal aging. Recollections and remembrances arose alongside newly formed questions about mortality and the meaning of life.

I believe the drive to record these impressions and discoveries rests in what Scott Russell Sanders suggests as a natural desire to consider one's life and to consider it in relationship to others: family, community, nature, and world; and in an inherent instinct for survival and growth.[6] Without the *élan vital*—the creative force within an organism that is responsible for growth, change, and necessary or desirable adaptations—stasis settles in. So, as Parker J. Palmer suggests, as I stand on the "brink of everything," the horizon poses a choice: relinquishing to a personal desuetude or an opportunity for renewed life.

In response to these compelling forces, I reached for a pen to tell the stories herein—the manifestation of spirit, *élan vital* at work when I'm moved to take note of the sleek gait of the elk, the still of a heavy snow, and the pink, salmon and white light of autumn's eve. I conclude the stirring is an evocation of the soul speaking, the soul tapping, beckoning me not only to meet change and loss with hope and trust, but ask the question of which Mark Nepo writes, "What instrument will I be?"[7] as I carry on and embrace this precious and mortal life.

Elk River Valley

ONE

Denizen

Tell me the landscape in which you live, and I will tell you who you are.

—Jose' Ortega y Gasset

WAS ONCE TOLD THAT THE LANDSCAPE IN WHICH YOU WERE born remains with you as though imprinted deep in the newborn brain. I was born on the high plains of Santa Barbara, Chihuahua, Mexico. But I've never desired a return to dry high ground. My first fondness for a landscape was as a child, wishing I were Heidi in the children's story by the same name. In my mind, she lived in the perfect wonderland: orphaned and living with her paternal grandfather in the Swiss Alps. Whatever potency the early imprint may or may not have made in Mexico, that first draw to an alpine landscape never left me.

For nearly forty years, I've lived on a ranch in northwestern Colorado within minutes of snow-covered mountains and a rugged continental divide. When they're in sight, I imagine that I possess their strength and, for an instant, their immortality. The Elk River runs not far from my bedroom window, and when I hear it at night, I'm soothed by its presence. In the blue spruce forest and aspen groves where I wander, I never fail to hear Ralph Waldo Emerson's words: "In the woods, we return to reason and faith."[8] And in the valley, the open meadowlands most often ring out to me as though to say, "Anything is possible."

I'm intrigued with the idea that landscape is an inherent creator of who we are and become. When reading *Bone Deep in Landscape:*

Writing, Reading, and Place, by Mary Clearman Blew, in which she suggests that "place affects our innermost selves," I was drawn to another reference in her writing. Barry Lopez, who in *Home Ground: Language for an American Landscape,* writes "our minds are shaped by landscape . . . interior landscape is a metaphorical representation of exterior landscape." If my landscape takes up residence within, what exactly resides inside?

Our life in the Elk River Valley is an agricultural one tied to the basic elements of climate, soil, and vegetation; and we, too, are socially embedded in a small rural community. Those who study cultural landscapes define these elements as forces in the creation of human activity specific to the physical environment and the identity that follows from the nature of the work and necessities of daily life.

T. H. Gaster, a theologian, coined *topocosm* from the Greek— *topo* for place and *cosmos* for world order. Deep ecologists refer to topocosm as the order of a place, the entire complex of any given locality conceived as a living organism—not just the human community but the total community—the plants, animals, and soils of the place.

The life my husband, Pete, and I live is ordered in so many ways by the light. Not unlike native societies who honored seasonal rituals rooted in the winter and summer solstices and the spring and fall equinoxes, our tie to place follows the cycles of the sun. When the northern hemisphere tilts toward the sun, our work year begins.

With a sun rising come spring, we time our breeding year to usher in newborn foals in May and June. In July, as the summer sends out it fieriest flames, mowers roll out across the valley, the hay drying in its surrender. As the evenings cool, the gathering begins. Wood, summer tools, the baler, the mower, and the rake—all tucked away. Cows gathered off the meadows; calves weaned, brand inspected and shipped, the practical cycles following the sun.

While the landscape does not physically nourish me—I do not browse the hill with the elk or search for prey like the coyote—I am nurtured by its acquaintance and over the years, its intimacy. I know when the first stand of aspens on Elk Mountain turns to gold. In late July, I know that the river nearby will quiet, and I'll no longer hear its lullaby at night. I'm aware that the greater sage grouse walks alongside me, inconspicuous in the bush, until it flees its camouflage, the sound of its take-off like a child's pull to rip the seams of a birthday gift.

However, as familiar as I feel, life in my natural habitat might surprise me too. An old, gnarly growth in the oak in the middle of winter can fool me at first glance. Instead, I find it's a portly porcupine balanced in the branches, nibbling. Later, I see his tracks in the snow like a turtle returning to the sea. Yesterday, the pine squirrel, its outstretched arm motionless in the mid-gather of acorns for his stash, appeared a bronze cast perched on the rugged branch. In his frozen pose, he thought himself invisible, a secret in his young fur coat the color of bare oak, his outline, a sketch along the trail. These inhabitants, these denizens infuse my world.

The first time I came across the word "denizen," I imagined a storybook scene of squirrels, rabbits, and friendly raccoons blissful in their repose, the forest a sweet backdrop. However, the curious word had a sophisticated ring, as though it meant more than creatures simply wandering the woods. In the next moment the scene shifted in my mind, and I envisioned the furry denizens moving deeper into the thicket as though they were indwellers, inhabitants, merging with the woods, all akin.

A denizen, self-selected as I or biologically adapted, naturalizes within a habitat. Something in the meeting between the light and shade, the contours of unyielding yet soft earth, the water's rise and fall suits the inhabitant over time, the elements making life possible, sustainable. I am a denizen—a dweller, an inhabitant, an occupant, a local.

> *The landscapes we know and return to become places of solace. We are drawn to them because of the stories they tell, because of the memories they hold, or simply because of the sheer beauty that calls us back again and again.*[9]
>
> —Terry Tempest Williams

After snow-shoeing to the top of a nearby hillside on the ranch, our dogs Emma, a Boston terrier, and Griz, a Blue Heeler-Border Collie cross, and I linger. We follow our own rituals when we arrive. If the winds are quiet, Griz and Emma hunt for scents among the sagebrush, perhaps noting whether a coyote or fox or elk had traveled over the ridge. On other days when the winds out of the west rustle my jacket, Emma and Griz stand at my feet; Emma's eyes settle on the track headed back home, and Griz turns away from the snowstorm rushing through Long Gulch.

Today, the winds whistle, and my ritual begins. In familiar phrases, I repeat the names of the landmarks marking the terrain. In between blinks, a kind of snowflake dodge ball, I imagine the Elk River Valley below and the rugged edge of the Zirkel Wilderness to the northwest hidden beneath low-lying clouds.

In my mind's eye I follow the Elk River as it meanders, crisscrossing meadow lands where our cattle and horses feed before it turns east out of view near Red Dirt Trail. Then to the south, I scan Elk Mountain standing unchallenged, a sentry at the foot of the valley floor. Soon Long Gulch draws my eye to the west, its rolling hills inhabited every quarter mile with a neighbor's home.

In the recitation, an incantation of the contours of my home, a home I've come to know. A home now imprinted, not just a backdrop, but a living landscape fused into my heart.

Emma shakes beneath her coat as the storm pushes east across the summit. It's time to descend. Reluctant, I set out onto the trail. In the first few steps, I carry a ticker tape filled with images: the Zirkel's cloudy shroud; a curling band of mother cows feeding in the meadow; a cottonwood-lined Elk River disappearing into the valley's end; a stalwart Elk Mountain; and my extended neighborhood nestled in the hillsides of Long Gulch.

A creature of habit, I tuck away the landscape as if it were my very own possession and follow Emma and Griz on down the trail toward home.

The earliest maps were "story" maps. Cartographers were artists who mingled knowledge with supposition, memory and fears. Their maps described both landscape and the events, which had taken place within it, enabling travellers to plot a route as well as to experience a story.[10]

—Rory MacLean

And just as I feel comfort in the natural world of my home, the physical landscape sets a textured backdrop for story: a narrative of both the daily comings and goings, and the vagaries of our rural life.

The corner gate at the base of the hill, a small triangle of land we own but share with adjacent landowners for access to property and water, became grounds for a five-year legal battle. A Texan purchased over 800 nearby acres without access to his new property.

Upon arrival, he trespassed, drew up legal papers, and sued us and two other ranchers—at significant expense to us all—for access he felt entitled to. A belief in the right to do whatever one wants, and in this case, forcing others to defend what is already legally theirs, ripped at the fabric of our neighborhood. After five years of legal wrangling, the Texan gained access through a neighboring rancher's property. We were relieved it wasn't through our ranch property even though the relief came at our own personal expense.

The lower meadow, once home to elk cows and calves, now hosts geldings and mares for summer day pasture. Our hopeful venture to diversify our ranching operation by raising domestic elk for meat ended with the rising cost of producing and processing the animals. The added cost included the required testing of the animal's brain stem at Colorado State University labs for chronic wasting disease, found in deer and elk. Like mad cow disease, chronic wasting disease affects the nervous system and brain, which are attacked by prions, infectious proteins.

Forced to disperse the herd because there was no longer a viable market, we ached when we advertised the last of our herd to hunters. We silently wept with regret when each one triumphed as they "bagged" their elk from across the meadow, knelt by the antler rack for a photo for the folks back home. They appeared to believe they had truly "hunted" their big game, and most took the animals, not for the meat, but for the rack or the hide.

Other spaces carried story too: the physical settings of our social landscape, the one in which we threaded the heart of our relational lives. The Moonhill School House—where both my children sat on Santa's lap for the first time; and where a community quilt I contributed to with other young local mothers still hangs on the wall—remains a community gathering place for potlucks, yoga, and neighborhood meetings.

And at the Clark Store, complete with post office, library, liquor store, grocery store, and deli, the cashier, Chris, always sets aside a Sunday paper for me to pick up when I arrive. Diego at the deli asks me, "So, Miss Mary, the regular? A breakfast sandwich on brioche or on the side, today?" And near the library, another Mary, a woman in her fifties, planning her next trip to Africa where she's helped save young women from genital mutilation and early marriage. She catches me, "Hey, Mary, how's it's going? How's that grandbaby? Have a minute? I'll show you the girls' graduation."

I believe Mary Clearman Blew is correct. Geography becomes personal when we find the place we feel at home—city, coast, plains, hillsides, or arid land. In whatever way a young mind works, I knew instinctively the high mountains of Heidi, not a high desert, felt like home. I consider myself tucked in snug here, with the evergreen and cottonwood, the open meadows and snow-covered divides. Tied to the familiar, the other, and embedded memories, I see my reflection in the physical world affirmed.

I walk out across the meadow to the hill, my hill. I ascend. A faint rise of heat comes from the ground beneath my feet. The chokecherry and sarvisberry bushes lining the utility road hang with fruit. Each step feels reverent. The air earthy, organic, thick-leafed, all melding, infusing one and the other. I stand in the middle of the draft lifted, at home.

TWO

THE HEARTSEASE
OF LONG GULCH

WHEN THE CHATTER OF MY DAILY LIFE SLIPS INTO a din, I often walk down our county road. Heading first south, County Road 56 intersects our ranch before it turns west through the heart of Long Gulch where it cooperates with the terrain like an old walking path.

I'm usually not alone. I'm accompanied by my loyal companions, Emma and Griz. We've walked together for a decade. Emma leads the pack, and Griz follows from behind, ever the herding dog. My companions are each the dog of our lifetimes, so the saying goes, one spirit connecting in a way no other animal has. My dog, Emma, believes she can do anything. In the drive, a strong will I admire. Griz, Pete's dog, is a fierce, if need be, lover boy. Pete knows he'll never have another Grizzly Bear. So, when we travel together, we're a tight-knit trio: we intuit the other, we protect the other.

As we go, Emma and Griz sniff the road for changes in the landscape since our last outing: maybe the scent of a fox, an ermine, a deer, or an elk who passed by during the night. I follow their lead. Last winter I watched a porcupine living up above the road in tall oak brush. He ate his way through the winter on the bark and twigs of old scrub oak. I often watch, too, for the snowshoe rabbits. They're thick this year, their tracks running along the side of the road like toddlers' footprints in shoes.

After hitting a rhythmical stride, I look to Elk Mountain, ten miles away to the south. The Ute people, who summered in northwestern Colorado for the healing powers of the hot springs, called it Sleeping

Giant. The profile of the mountain from the south suggests a Ute Chief at rest on his back, his arms across his chest, his feet relaxed. Then as we ease into Long Gulch, I welcome the largesse of the open road—its peace, its unencumbered space, the small rise of oak and sage-covered hills rimming my way.

Each time I enter in I struggle to name what the open landscape says to my heart. Even though I don't believe in a personal Christian god, I do sense an invitation to lay down whatever is puzzling or troubling to me as though I had wandered into a sanctuary. On days when it's difficult to accept the invitation, the weight of the burden of whatever I carry still feels lightened, if only for a few precious moments.

Occasionally, our journey is interrupted by familiar vehicles and friends passing by. I'm proud to say that when others pass, we are a safe and congenial group on the road. Both dogs know that when they hear or see an oncoming vehicle, they are to return to me, to sit and wait. So, it's with peace of mind we often meet regulars like Bill, the mailman; contractors in pickups sometimes hauling low boys with heavy equipment; Art, the UPS man; and in the summer, ranchers driving tractors and bale wagons.

During much of the last thirty years, the neighborhood and the road have remained relatively quiet. Only recently has Long Gulch filled in. Families, couples, and retirees have settled into small acreages of hay meadow and the unassuming development of Buck Mountain. With new neighbors commuting to work, mothers taking children to our local charter school, and heavy construction traffic, the ease of the road has changed.

Our walks were without incident until a few years ago when a small white Toyota pickup came upon us at a very high rate of speed. I didn't see or hear him coming until the last minute. I tried frantically to wave him down, so I could gather up Emma, Griz. I feared he'd run over Emma who is the least likely to get out of the way. Griz would take care of himself. But the driver didn't make any attempt to move over or slow down.

I felt an old protective mother bear roar inside. I cursed and shouted at him, "You stupid son of a bitch! You could have killed my dogs!" But the words simply sailed on down the road. Whatever the driver saw ahead of him apparently didn't register as a human being with dogs on the side of the road. Even though I couldn't identify the driver, I knew he wasn't like the neighbors I've come to know as friends. They slow down. They move over. They say, "Hello!"

One February afternoon, my neighbor, Ann, who knows how

to plumb, set a foundation, repair snowmobiles, and preserve chokecherry jelly, stops by in her maroon GMC. Dressed in a Carhart work jacket and her gray hair customarily pulled back, she eagerly says, "I had to tell you I spotted the first bluebird the other day. I think it's the earliest I've ever seen one here."

"Makes me worry. Does it you?"

"Heck yeah," she laughs as though to say everyone's crazy if they don't take notice of the changes in our natural world.

Not one to talk too long, Ann doesn't linger but heads on into town. Some days she picks up her granddaughter for a day back at grandma's, riding the ATV, feeding the horses, and picking chokecherries for grandma's crimson jelly.

When a little royal blue pickup or dark gray diesel truck with a horse trailer approaches, I know it's my longtime neighbor, Jerry, a retired physical therapist with a short, no-nonsense haircut and easy laugh. In the driver's seat is her friend Larry, dressed in a work shirt, home to his customary suspenders. Larry grew up in the valley and knows most everyone. Beneath a loyal and well-worn straw cowboy hat, there's a weathered and friendly face. In retirement he and Jerry look for reasons to ride and be of help. They ride most every day, either on the trail or helping Larry's son and daughter on their ranches nearby, usually gathering or doctoring cattle.

Whenever he comes along, he slows way down. When I thank him for watching out for us, he says, "I don't want anything to happen. I know when I've got dogs with me, your dogs might want to jump in." Larry's a tough cowboy who knows what a good dog means to its owner: a right hand in gathering summering cows, a watchman, a close comfort at night. He also knows how quickly an accident can take the partnership away.

County Road 56 has been a thoroughfare since the turn of the century. When the silver and gold mines north in Hahn's Peak failed to produce, settlers and pioneers took up homesteads on fertile hay meadows and grazing land down valley, creating the communities of Glen Eden, Clark, Moonhill, Long Gulch, and Deep Creek. Homesteaders Campbell, Drake, and Winkleman first claimed land in the Long Gulch neighborhood in the late nineteenth century. Then the ranching families of the Semotans, the Graves, and the Powells settled in along its length in the thirties and forties. Their homes still exist and two are inhabited by direct descendants.

In the early twentieth century, the *Steamboat Pilot* regularly reported the Long Gulch neighbors' comings and goings, whether it was for socializing or business. For example, "Special Correspondence from Long Gulch," October 25, 1916:

Ralph Drake and Bennett Savage shipped several car loads of cattle to Denver and Omaha Saturday. Ralph went with the cattle.

Anna Drake took dinner Sunday with Emma Cross.

Also, "Special Correspondence from Long Gulch," July 2, 1919:

Mr. and Mrs. Elmer Drake and son Virgil called at John Mosher's and Will Cross's Sunday afternoon.

H. E. Drake and family, W. D. Bowden and family, Henry Mosher and children, John Mosher and wife and C. P. Mosher motored to Glen Eden Sunday afternoon.

Jo Semotan, daughter of Quentin Semotan and still a resident of Long Gulch, made a similar report to me one afternoon from memories of her childhood in the forties: "When I was a girl, Daddy and Mommy packed fried chicken and potato salad in our saddle bags. We'd ride by horseback to that cottonwood halfway to your place. We'd meet neighbors there for a picnic in the shade on Sunday afternoons."

Quentin didn't have any sons and he expected Jo to do anything a boy would do growing up on the ranch. She learned the finer points of breeding quarter horses and cattle. Her father developed one of the early foundation quarter horses, Starduster, hauling him by truck and rail to Denver and Fort Worth for shows in the fifties and sixties.

Jo didn't think twice about saddling up to doctor a steer, gather up a herd, or help her dad blow up beaver damns with dynamite if the water wasn't flowing just right through their meadows. "Daddy thought I should be able to do anything, and I did." Jo went on to be a dancer, horse trainer, teacher, ski instructor, and mental health professional.

The cottonwood still stands tall on the side of the road, often with a magpie or crow sitting up high or our horses beneath it seeking its shade in August. Jo, now in her seventies, and her daughter still host holiday parties at the Semotan ranch. Everyone is welcome.

I don't see Jerry and Larry as often as I used to. They bought a horse place in Arizona where Jerry's father lived and where they now winter over. I do catch up once they're back in March. When they stop, Larry, whose eyes never fail to light up, says, "Yeah, we're sure glad we weren't here this winter. Heard you guys got hit." Then Jerry talks about how hard it was to lose her father that winter even though she knew he'd had a good, long life.

But one of those spring days when they came back up north, I asked Larry what could be done about the speeding on our road. He said, "I don't know. We told Kurtis, (a local deputy) about it, but it didn't do any good."

Then I told Larry and Jerry I'd discovered who the driver of the white Toyota pickup was. I'd seen his vehicle going into a neighbor's ranch where the owners were remodeling. So I inquired. They said, "Yeah, that's John, he's working on our house."

Another neighbor knew about John too. He races down a long straightaway in front of her home at the end of the day. She told him about her concern at a local barbecue. But he didn't care. With a laugh, he said, "I just like to drive fast." In his answer one might suspect a teenager.

Even though I had suspected the driver to be a newcomer, John had lived west of our home for nearly forty years. He was a sixty-something father of a young adult son. I had never seen John on County Road 56 until 2013. As a construction worker, the circumstances of his commute shifted and required that he drive down our road and head north rather than down County Road 54 and south into town.

But I wondered why he believed he had a right to do whatever he wanted even though it put others in danger? Was it part western independence gone awry or lack of empathy? And if so, what interfered with his understanding? Was he once a child dismissed, a child mistreated?

His speeding white truck was an offensive break-in into the sanctuary of the natural and communal world of Long Gulch. The driver, the intruder, disrupted a peace he had no right to disrupt. I mourned the loss and then I protested the loss.

I called the county road department.

I requested they at least post the speed limit. They agreed, and six months later County Road 56 is posted at thirty-five miles per hour and our blind driveways highlighted with a cautionary speed of twenty miles per hour.

And then, my anger took another turn. One late summer afternoon I watched my daughter-in-law head out to walk my granddaughter down the road. The speeding commuter may be on his way home at the same time. I watch, holding my breath. Surely John will slow as he passes by. He did not. Dust flew. He rounded the corner and I ran for the phone. I called the sheriff.

Mark, the deputy on staff that day, had a kind ear. He took my report and concern seriously. I knew the name of the driver, the make and model of his truck, his license number, and his place of residence. The deputy couldn't ticket the driver for what I had long considered reckless driving, but my report went on his record and any further documentation could lead to a citation. Mark also said he would personally serve him with a warning at his home.

Looking back, I have likened my protest to the spirit in which Scott Russell Sanders writes in his essay, "Staying Put," from *Earth Works*.[11]

> *If our fidelity to place is to help renew and preserve our neighborhoods, it will have to be informed by what Wendell Berry in* Standing by Words *calls "an ecological intelligence: a sense of the impossibility of acting or living alone or solely on one's own behalf, and this rests in turn upon a sense of the order upon which any life depends and of the proprieties of place within that order. Proprieties of place: actions, words, and values that are proper to your home ground."*

Four days after my call to the sheriff, I receive a phone call from the driver of the white pickup. He hears I'm concerned about his driving and wonders what the problem is. I list the encounters we'd had with him in the years he'd driven our road.

"You know, the first time you came by me, I tried to wave you down because I didn't have my dogs rounded up. You didn't even slow down. When my son came back to the ranch to live, he asked me, 'Who in the hell drives that white pickup?' Our hired hand said, 'Yeah, that guy came down the straight-a-way so fast he ended up in the driveway across the road to avoid hitting me in the tractor.' And Pete's watched you fly by and put him and other drivers in dangerous situations when he's turned into the center gate."

John replies, "Well, you're kind of a skittish bunch, aren't you.?"

With a deep breath I hope he hears over the phone, "You know, there's a real disconnect here. There's a problem and the sheriff knows all about it."

In a blink, as though the scene shifts in a movie, John, the driver of the white pickup, says, "Yeah, you're right. I'm sorry about what I did."

I don't know what moves him to apologize. Perhaps, he'd been directed by Mark. But I accept his apology, and when I do, he respectfully says, "I'm honored you accepted my apology." I'm not sure of his sincerity, but I want to be thankful and sincere in return. Time will tell if he really means what he says.

So before we hang up, I invite the driver of the white pickup truck to stop next time he sees me out for a walk on the road. I tell him I'd like to say "Hi!" And so, he does. A month or so later, he slows to a stop and rolls down his window. "You're Mary, right? John here." A man in his mid-sixties, his beard, a mix of gray and blond, his hands thick from construction work, and his blue eyes tentative yet not shying away. We shake hands and as we visit, I learn he makes an annual pilgrimage each July to the Wind River Range in Wyoming with family and friends. They pack in on horseback for ten days. He's been doing it for seventeen years.

I had cursed John, the driver of the white pickup, for four years. Whatever turned his sense of entitlement to one of cooperation, I'm not sure I'll ever know, nor do I know for sure he'll continue to care. But I am grateful for now. John and I came to know one another in the simplest of ways when we looked one another in the eye. I believe in those briefest of moments when we see and are seen, when we acknowledge the presence of others through the smallest daily ritual of communications on a ribbon of road, a simple narrative forms and contributes to the sacred fabric of our communal lives.

THREE

Fireweed

T HE PLUME OF SMOKE APPEARED TO BE NEARBY, AS THOUGH it were burning on nearby Buck Mountain. We wondered, could it come our way, burning our meadows, buildings, and home? The plume, already several hundred feet high, was white with periodic flares of dark smoke. We called 911.

Clips from news stories about wildfires in California flashed in and out of my mind. Was it our turn? Could this fire burn its way to the horse arena where my son works? Would we have to evacuate? I'd always kept the possibility compartmentalized, tucked away as though we were immune.

I hopped in the car with my sister, who was visiting, and drove west to find out how close those dark plumes were. She and I had faced fires of another kind as we cared for our mother for eight years until her death. A kind of combustion took place whenever our mother's needs weren't being met, and we had to advocate for proper food, medication, or appropriate nursing home attention and care. So somehow driving to assess a wildfire was not unlike our team approach to our mother's care.

But it was with relief we rounded the corner on our county road and saw the wildfire well beyond our neighborhood, perhaps fifteen to twenty miles away near California Park, a popular hunting area. I entertained the question again, though, as I surveyed the plume. Could we eventually be at risk if high winds blew in the right direction? Could the wildfire burn hay meadow and sage and all the way to our home?

According to Steve Pyne in "Moved by Fire: History's Promethean Moment," fire is older than insects, trees, and Pangaea, the supercontinent consisting of all seven continents interconnected. When hominins first discovered how to manipulate fire, approximately 600,000 years ago, their ability to cook catapulted them into the genus *Homo* by accelerating evolution through higher caloric intake, less disease, and a wider variety of foodstuffs. Brain development followed and it appears fire and man "co-evolved," with fire functioning as a keystone process for *Homo sapiens'* existence and evolution.

From its earliest use, fire has played a role in ritual, destruction, heat, light, signaling, smelting, forging, incineration, cremation, and warfare—as a thermal weapon. It also formed the nexus of human social interaction in the communal fire, providing warmth, light, protection from predators, and eventually serving as the hearth metaphor for the heart of the home.

On occasional Thursday evenings in the fall and winter, after choir practice and before dinner when I was a child, my father would back his company pickup into the carport and direct me and my three siblings to unload his truck full of scrap wood. My father paid $0.50 and later $1 for his load from a lumber mill in Delta, Colorado, a small town he passed by on his travels as a uranium ore buyer in the fifties and sixties. The bark trimmings were what remained after milled timber had been sent through the saw mill.

We stacked the wood precisely against the carport wall. My father never liked an untidy world, whether it was his firewood or his pressed jeans and closet full of blue shirts. Even though we handled the equivalent of leftovers, each piece was cut at a given length so the stack, with our help, made its own order. Then on weekend nights or perhaps on a holiday in the basement of our subdivision home, my father would ask one of us to bring in a load of wood. He'd set the fire and light it with one match.

Sitting on the hearth I focused on the base of the fire where it ignited and burned steadily from the ligneous fuel. Whatever man knew about primal heat, I knew as a child: its mesmerizing and comforting heat, like the waves of the ocean, timeless. Not often did it turn back a chill. We lived in the western desert of the Colorado Plateau, and a fire wasn't often truly needed. But it always turned back a chill left in my home by my father's silence and distance. As I sat close to the fire, the lick and heat reassured.

Fire out of control on the ranch threatens our survival, but fire controlled on the ranch is a working tool. Before the meadow grasses rise in the spring and grow in earnest, when the cool air always reminds us that winter is not that far behind and could return, Pete packs a blow torch, a shovel, and a water sprayer in the John Deere Gator (ATV) and sets out to burn our irrigation ditches. Clearing the ditches is essential in making way for the spring runoff and a smooth flow of irrigation water. He must pick a day on which the breeze from the west and southwest is calm. The fire triangle he'll be working with—ignition, combustible material, and an adequate supply of oxygen—doesn't need any more encouragement to burn. When the smoke rises, I smell burning grass and soil and consistently worry about Pete losing control of the burn. It's never happened.

The closest we ever came to a catastrophic wildfire nearby was in 2002 when the Zirkel Wilderness caught fire by a lightning strike, burning 31,016 acres. Five years earlier the wilderness suffered a blowdown. Unusual early winter winds with the force of a hurricane downed six million trees and cleared a swath twenty miles long and several miles wide. In places, the remains were twenty feet high, including a pixie stick arrangement of snapped trees and root balls lifted in the air and dropped unceremoniously after the whipping winds passed through. The Zirkel Wilderness forest floor deep in combustible fuel laid in waiting.

At the fire's peak, the ridge to the east of the ranch raged and could be seen for miles. When I drove home from our country fair one evening, I captioned the scene in my mind—Hell on Earth. It was as though Mother Nature and the elements had made an executive decision to bring the world to an end. While it was deeply stirring, it was not an imminent threat to our ranch and home. But, as I recently hear reports from Paradise, California, I realize fire may not feel imminent but is. And hell on earth does devour homes and lives, and with it, I imagine faith and hope in the rightness of our natural world.

The conflagration my sister and I noticed, later named the Mill Creek Fire, had erupted behind Pilot's Knob in deep beetle kill lodgepole pine, spruce, and aspen forest. The necessary elements for a wildfire merged into a "fire triangle"—an ignition source in contact with combustible material and sufficient oxygen to fuel the chemical reaction. News reports said a contractor was clearing a fire line on private land with a bulldozer when a tree fell across the dozer. While the operator left to retrieve a chainsaw, the heat of the engine lit the tree on fire. Machinery is one of the main ignition sources in man-made fires. Where beetles laid out death and decay the lick of flames didn't waste any time moving through gray and bare lodgepole pine and old slash piles from earlier timbering. With growing heat and embers, the surviving healthy pines weren't any match for the winds of the inferno.

As I write, 460 acres have burned with the wildfire 30 percent contained, meaning a fire line has been established around 30 percent of the perimeter of the fire. One hundred thirty-five firefighters, a helicopter, and a slurry plane have been called to assist. One recent afternoon, the helicopter made a hundred runs with a bucket of water, called a Bambi Bucket, capable of carrying anywhere from 72 to 2,600 gallons of water and hanging hundreds of feet below its deck, refilled while in flight at a nearby water source.

We watched all afternoon, keeping a measured assessment of the strength of the Mill Creek Fire. I was grateful it wasn't nearer. I imagined the charred forests and, for a moment, grief for the loss of the landscape. I wondered how it is home owners, who must flee their homes in the middle of a wildfire, return to build again in the devastation of the land that's left behind. Are those left with the destruction of their home and their familiar woods propelled forward by deep hope?

Fireweed, *Chamaenerion angustiflolium,* also known as great willow herb and rosebay willow herb, a pioneering species native to the northern hemisphere, abundant in open fields, pastures, and especially burned-over lands. After a fire or disruption to the forest, the fireweed grows out of the devastation with plenty of light, coloring the wound of the landscape magenta to pink. As the trees renew, the plants die out, but plentiful seeds remain and when a new fire or disturbance occurs, the seeds germinate once again and bring hope and life back to the land.

In junior high, I asked my father, a mining engineer, what the blue flame was at the base of the candlelight. Surely, he knew. But, he said, "That's what you'll learn in high school chemistry," and turned away. I never did find out what caused the blue flame in high school chemistry.

Now I understand that the flame's color indicates the temperature of the flame and as it rises, the flame cools to yellow, then orange and red. At the base of the flame, the heat is highest, and when airborne soot is less concentrated, a candle flame burns blue at the base. The temperature of fire and flame vary with the quantity and quality of combustible material and the amount of available oxygen from the ambient air. A candle burns at 1,800 degrees, wood ignites at 1,000 degrees, and the deceased incinerate in a crematorium at 1,600–1,880 degrees.

I light a candle each evening before I begin cooking dinner. I began the ritual in 1997 after I visited Paris on an educational tour with my daughter. Walking the streets of Montmartre, I entered the Basilica of the Sacré-Cœur. There, I lit a candle for my grandmother, the first of many candles I light in remembrance. I continue with the ritual as I travel, recently in the Monte Senario, the Abbey of Sant' Antimo, and the Siena Cathedral. In the blue, yellow, orange, and red of the flame, I think of my late brother, my mother, my grandmother and grandfather. As I light the small votives, I remember the magic of lighting one advent wreath taper and imagine spirits rising and then resting in the peace of each holy place.

Fire, such a paradox, such a contradictory elemental element. It sustains life and all we know by heat, flame, and combustion. It forged man's evolution and civilization, made tools out of steel. Its flame illuminates the dark and the unknown, warms a hearth, regenerates the natural world, offers peace in candle light. Yet it devoured and destroyed—Paradise, California, and so many others, leaving hell on earth. Will the surviving souls rise and reseed, perhaps as fireweed amid the devastation? Will they know hope again in Paradise?

FOUR

A Fertile Foothold

MY MOTHER KNEW WILDFLOWERS. AFTER SHE STUDIED the artistic botanical depictions in her small volume, *Flowers: A Guide to Familiar American Wildflowers*, a Golden Nature Guide printed in 1950, she filed away their names and family assignment—geranium, buttercup, forget-me-not, sweet pea, and aster—with the memory of their brushed stroked replicas. The wildflower paperback still rests on my bookshelf with other volumes from my mother's library: *Birds of North America, The Roots of National Culture, Elements of Latin,* and her Bible, The New International Version. I have found since her death that her hunger for and curiosity about the world are with me, have never left me.

After staining our front porch one summer afternoon, I head out to one of my favorite trails on our ranch in northwestern Colorado. It winds its way up what we call the TV Tower, named after its signal equipment stationed on top. I've always found movement meditative, even though as a child I had no words for the peace I knew after playing hide-and-go-seek.

In preparation for the meditation, I slip on my running shoes, tie them snug. Fill my CamelBak full and check my mini-can of mace and bear bell. Amid my organizing, our dogs, Emma and Griz, spin and bark until they herd me out the door.

With a gentle June breeze coming in from the west, I head up the first small rise of the hillside. I ease into my ritual with slow steps. I greet the full bloom of the mule's ears and lupine lining my path. The broad, yellow smile of the mule's ears mimics a priest's offering, so hopeful, so free for the taking. The wild, silvery lupine, so much smaller than its domesticated relatives in my garden, asks for attention: close to the ground, their whorls stand only six to eight inches tall. In their short stature and presence on a dry, south-facing trail, I sense an undeterred will to be in the world.

Emma and Griz trot ahead in and out of young sage, sniffing under the oaks and along game trails. Sometimes I lose sight of them and call, "Emma Lou, Grizzly Bear!" They merge back on the trail, sometimes ahead of me and sometimes from behind, as if to say, "Just checking things out. No need to worry."

I usually don't worry about them, but recently, a yearling brown bear sauntered through my garden. The young bear, not yet sure of its commute to the river and back from its den on the hill, scurried through his detour as I watched from the kitchen window. And I spotted mountain lion tracks this winter. The paw imprints on the crest of the summit didn't belong, not in January. But the mild early winter kept the elk and deer nearby and so too the lion. The memory still lingers in June, as though the rush of my heart when I spotted the track persists, tucking itself into my primitive mind.

Once on top, a vertical climb of over eight hundred feet, our traveling pack seeks shade and a minute to catch our breath. I congratulate Griz on his climb with a rub of his ears. He looks as happy as the chiming bluebells beside him. Then I catch sight of the deep purple larkspur and the sticky geranium, its delicate pink a striking contrast to the rocky outcropping beneath our feet. I recognize the perennial bloom at the top of the hill. But while I recognize most of the wildflowers on the hill, I fail to know much about them.

I envied my mother's breadth of knowledge, not only about flowers, but about birds, history, religion, and world politics. In perusing the sweet June bloom, I remember the inadequacy I felt as an adolescent in my mother's shadow; yet, I remember too how, over time, I had worked to discover myself and who I was apart from her. In the small space of that moment with Griz at my feet, I gratefully held the memory and the earned ease of my adult sense of self.

Now, after her death, I'm aware I stay connected to her through her love of the world. So, like the silvery little lupine, I was undeterred in wanting to know about the wildflower bloom. As soon as I came home, I researched each wildflower story, beginning with the *Wyethia x magna.*

Mule's Ears

Wyethia x magna, a genus of the sunflower family, also known as aster (*Asteraceae*)

In 1833, seekers Nathaniel Jarvis Wyeth, a Massachusetts merchant who in 1832 traveled by land to Oregon, and Thomas Nuttall, a highly praised botanist, explorer, and Harvard teacher, collected the common mountain sunflower. In his explorations with Wyeth, Nuttall collected and identified 113 western plants, including the sagebrush, *Artemisia tridentata,* and the mule's ears, a sunflower genus. In 1934, Nuttall named the mule's ear after Wyeth, christening it *Wyethia x magna.*

Each spring I eagerly greet the optimism of this misnamed plant. It is misnamed, isn't it? Mule's ears. What comes to mind if you hadn't seen it? Brown, shaggy, gangly, comical, perhaps? But it's not the mule's ears leaves I gladly let wash over me when the sunflower arrives on the earthen rise in June. It's the disposition I wish I carried all day long as they do. So sunny, cheered, and enthused. It's as though each blossom were that priest I mentioned, the one whose calm and faith imbues each parishioner as he or she passes by.

My mother carried this kind of faith. While I know she was not without her deep grief and, at times, a questioning of her belief, she, at the beginning and end of each day, infused her life with prayers of gratitude and hope. How I wish I had this kind of steadiness in the dailyness of my life.

Bluebell

Mertensia fusiformis, genus of the forget-me-not family

Edward Greene, both a botanist and an Episcopal priest, named over 4,400 new species of plants in the American West. In 1899 he christened the bluebell the *Mertensia fusiformis.* Tinges of pink sweeten the bell-like blossom of the bluebell. The bulb of the plant produces contractile roots; when these roots contract, they draw the bulb down deeper into layers of moisture soil. This is vital to the chiming bluebell's survival on this rocky upper hillside because it would prefer a wet river bank, marsh, or moist lowland.

I am taken by the innocence of the forget-me-not. It sways so easily in the breeze, moved by the spirit of rising thermals. Its belled clusters suggest an easy companionship, one with the other. What negotiations directed the roots to seek the dark moist soil, the soil beneath the crumble and burial of old volcanic rock? What faith secured their belief in seeking their own survival together?

In the midst of my childhood and adolescence, my mother struggled to care for her four children and my father's ever deepening depression. Under the weight, she survived with a stoicism most would never truly comprehend.

In addition to her faith, I believe my mother's intellect, her thirst for knowledge and understanding, steadied her. It served as a point of return from the challenges of my father's dark life, a place in which she could remember who she was and what she so loved about the world. I'm aware I, too, follow in her footsteps. When the winds blow through my life, I return to my books and my desk to order my world.

Larkspur

Delphinium nuttallianum, genus of the buttercup family, *Ranunculaceae*

The common name, larkspur, comes from a spur-like projection on the rear of the flower. I've always known it's toxic to grazing cattle if enough of the plant is ingested, causing neuromuscular paralysis and eventual respiratory failure. But I didn't know it also created beauty in the lives of indigenous people. Native Americans used the blue juice of the larkspur as coloring dye for arrows and other ceremonial items. Among the sixty native larkspur species in the United States, this is the Nuttall larkspur, another plant first discovered by Nuttall on his expedition with Wyeth near the Columbia River in 1834.

Poison and beauty embodied in one, all in the same cellular structures. I lean into the larkspur as a trope for life and wish it were easy to say I accept that light and dark are not one without the other.

My mother often said, "Just because you're a Christian doesn't mean a little rain won't fall on your life." I understand the original line was penned by Longfellow in 1842 and made more popular in 1944 by the Ink Spots, featuring Ella Fitzgerald and Bill Kenny. But as a child, I took it as biblical scripture. In researching this notion, I discovered a passage most closely resembling the dictum: "In the world you will have tribulation; but be of good cheer, I have overcome the world." (John 16:33 NKJV)

At eight, my mother was instructing me on facing and accepting the reality of the light and dark in life. Being a believer is important, but it doesn't protect you from the vagaries of mortal life. It was a turning moment in my young life when she began quoting this phrase. Until then, I had always felt secure in the belief that if I believed in God, all good things would come my way.

Sticky Geranium

Geranium viscosissimum (sticky geranium, sticky cranesbill), genus of the geranium family, *Geraniaceae*

The sticky pink geranium was used medicinally by the Blackfeet Indians and other Native Americans. It transforms itself into a doctor's little black bag. From infusions for gastric upset, colds, and sore throats to powdered astringents for the treatment of external bleeding, what comfort this petite pink plant has offered. Also used today as an attractive garnish for salads, its deep red and purple veins capture the eye and perhaps in the same way it captured the imagination of the Blackfeet who discovered it in the grasslands and forests of Montana.

In the garden off the kitchen deck, my domestic geraniums surface beneath the *Rosa rugosa*. As though an understudy or minor character in summer days on the ranch, they settle in their place beneath the petite yellow rose without any need to impress. Sometimes I wish these deeper purple geraniums were laced with pink like the sticky geranium that Griz rests nearby when we summit the ridge.

When I wish in this way, I'm reminded of an old wise offering: to state one's desires as preferences rather than necessities lightens one's heart and mind. In the shift, the mind winds its way out of the hard-sided rut when any given object, event, person, stoplight, or grocery store line must be a certain way. The rocky terrain of necessities eases when the need softens, and in the transformation— detachment, freedom.

I hear a Buddhist monk in the words I have just written. I am not a Buddhist. I am not the Presbyterian my mother raised me to be. And some days I wish I were for I cannot define what it is I believe. I only know I am drawn over and again to faith, to the sounds of the organ of my childhood church, to a spiritual presence in my daily life. I find it most often in the natural world, in the intimacy of relationship, and in the complexity of life itself.

It must have been disappointing to my mother that I did not remain a Presbyterian. But she never mentioned it. She never said, "Why don't you get back to the church? You know it would be good for you." My mother's desire became a preference, and then the preference transformed into full relinquishment and acceptance of who I was. I wish she had said more about the letting go of her desire.

Silvery Lupine

Lupinus argenteus (silvery lupine), a genus of flowering plants in the legume family, *Fabaceae*

Early Egyptian and pre-Incan people consumed the lupine seed, a source of protein, throughout the Mediterranean region and the Andean mountains for three to six thousand years. Roman agriculturalists knew the plant for its ability to improve the fertility of soils. Its tolerance for barren and infertile soils combined with its ability to fertilize the soil establishes a foothold not only for the lupine, but for other plants.

The lupine claims a "plant homestead," making the infertile fertile and the inhospitable hospitable. The lupine, a pioneering plant of sorts—scout, pathfinder, trailblazer, colonist, and guide. The pioneers whose imaginations pushed against the stony West established a foothold, a shelter, a source of water, and food.

In the silvery lupine I sense an undeterred will to be in the world. And so, it's true. What I saw on the trail in the silvery lupine is indeed a life force driven to survive, a life force determined to blaze a trail, guide, make a foothold for those to follow.

As I bore witness to the last days of my mother's life, I watched the drive to life she had carried with her so fervently leave her. I rebelled against the fact. But in the failing of her body and mind, I also knew she, in her faith, was relinquishing, letting go, and in doing so embracing what she believed to be eternal life.

My mother's death was a peaceful one. My sister and I turned to her New International Version of the Bible and read from the Psalms during the last minutes of her life. I opened a window to set her spirit free—a Danish custom upon death. And there we remained, motherless, but not without a foothold, a fertile home in our hearts and minds that she had carved out for us.

FIVE

MIGRATIONS

A GAME PATH CROSSES THE HILLSIDE BELOW THE HEM OF the aspens where the spring runs all year. It's there that I often wonder what sets the wildlife in motion when the seasons change. Some leave and some stay behind. If they migrate, how is it they know where to go? If they stay, how do they find winter shelter? And as spring peeks out, how do those who left decide whether to go back home?

Bracketed to a tall post by a friend of ours, a game camera tracks their comings and goings all year. This year's flash drive revealed a robust herd of elk, more than in recent years; multiple black bears, young and old alike; two sightings of mountain lion, which we see only occasionally; and most surprising, a bobcat this year. They all sip from the spring. The bears often sit in the water tank where the enduring spring collects as though they're at the pool. Frequently, one or two young cubs will soak and splash together like siblings.

I discover that movement from place to place, while central to migration, has a specific purpose depending upon who or what is in motion and why. Animals travel from one region or climate to another primarily for food and shelter. Mankind has been restless, moving and resettling from his beginnings in Africa.

Beyond exploration of the world, he, too, has been driven by conflict and/or the need for food and shelter, often dictated by climatic conditions or changes in the landscape like the lowering of the seas or receding of glaciers. Those who migrate in this way today are referred to as climate refugees. In 2013 nearly "three times as many people were displaced by disasters than conflict." It's also recognized that "climate change serves as a 'threat multiplier' as food and water insecurity and competition over resources provoke or exacerbate conflict and compound displacement."[12]

How many disparate journeys there are. Some out of seed and instinct. Some by dream.

migrate: v., to pass periodically from one region or climate to another, as certain birds, fishes, and animals

Come November we watch the small elk and deer herds migrate from the higher elevation of the hill to the valley floor, gathering along the cottonwood-lined river, protected from the wind, feeding on the bark of the trees.

The black bears remain, this ground their home ground. They prepare for the winter by collecting serviceberries and chokecherries, nuts and seeds, and then they hibernate on the sheltered north side of the hill, deep in the aspen and evergreen.

The range of the mountain lion is three hundred miles. I've heard they most often move out of our country in the fall and head to eastern Utah where lion hunters tree them in the juniper. But I've also seen lion tracks in January and March. Our local wildlife officer told me they had lingered here because of a mild early winter. We've never seen a bobcat here, but I'm sure I followed its track one year as I snowshoed up the trail. And there are more— the crane and the hummingbird; the snowshoe rabbit; and in the dark, the vole.

Not all animal migratory behavior is yet fully understood, but most migration is driven by the weather and the access to food stores. Creatures of all kinds use a mental map with a legend made up of landmarks—rivers, trees, mountains— the wind, sun, moon, and stars, and the senses of sound, smell, and the feel of the wind. So it follows that the nearby elk and deer herds have an easy go of it. They wander to a familiar landscape when the weather shifts, following the tracks of previous generations, settling on the river where there's food and protection in the willows and cottonwoods.

Although the black bear hibernates, its range can cover well over one hundred miles and it's not understood how they manage to return home. It's also not clear what cue prompts the mother bear to emerge in the spring with her young. On average, when the cubs reach three months of age, they wander out into the world.

Mountain lions appear to use a sense of smell and attunement to temperature to find an easier winter climate, one of drier ground and easier access to prey. The greater sandhill crane uses visual cues such as familiar mountains, rivers, and valleys to guide their route. Hummingbirds respond to the number of hours of sunlight at a certain time of year and use cues from the earth's magnetic field. They use the sun position in the sky as a compass. They recall landmarks such as rivers, coastlines, mountain ranges, and even highways.

And the snowshoe rabbit and voles don't migrate or hibernate. Snowshoe rabbits remain in their home range of approximately twenty acres. They rest in dens during the day and venture out at night, surviving on marginal winter foodstuffs that include willows and sarvisberry. Voles survive the winter months by constructing a labyrinth of snow tunnels. The tunnels provide a steady environment protecting these animals from the normal fluctuations of cold and wind.

migrate: v., to go, move, travel, resettle, relocate

As I imagine the wintering habits of our resident wildlife, I'm reminded that man, too, has traveled to, come and gone here hundreds of years. The Utes moved as the weather changed seasonally, summering in the Yampa Valley, hunting in the hills, healing in nearby medicinal hot springs and then returning to winter-over in Utah. Their journey followed game trails and landmarks, like the Bears Ears Butte, signaling the near end of their journey when they traveled east in the spring.

Following the footfall of the Utes and other Native Americans to northwestern Colorado, miners migrated to Routt County on word of gold and silver in hills of Hahn's Peak in the 19th c. 10,000 souls settled in, seeking resources of the land with which to build and sustain a life. Like the black bear, hardy miners and their families wintered over, tucked into small log cabins, staying alive on stores of elk and deer and warmed by deep stacks of fire wood.

When the promises of wealth died out, the next migration of pioneers, those willing to shift their focus, their enterprise, began when word of fertile hay ground and rich grazing land brought those seeking a homestead of 160 acres, food, shelter and home ground for succeeding generations.

migrate: v., to shift, as from one system, mode of operation, or enterprise to another

In a lifetime, one might migrate toward a dream or aspiration, from one focus, sense of purpose, or way of doing or thinking, to another. From place to place we can be moved out of a need for something certain and important to our survival in some fundamental way. Could it be, when we are moved in this way, that we are not unlike the sun migrating at daybreak, rising over the Zirkel Wilderness, traveling to the western horizon and hills of Deep Creek, on to the eastern desert of Utah, the Great Basin and beyond? Its movement changing the focus of night into day; its purpose, to warm and light.

While both Pete and I grew up on the edge of the desert in western Colorado, we both, from a young age, were moved by and loved a mountainous landscape and the vibrancy of a year of seasons. How is it that children know these things on their own? What stars speak to them?

When we arrived in 1979, we'd searched the valley for two years, returning to explore thoughts of leaving our home behind and settling into a new place. How would we fare? Could we return if our decision had been misguided, the wind direction misinterpreted, cues from our internal compass amiss?

We, like the early settlers, used maps and news of those who had gone before us. As we searched for a different life, a place we could raise our family and thrive, the map we held in our hands, in hindsight, had a personalized legend.

In 1977, a small dot on the map, indicating a small town, confirms our desire. Then we look, not for solid black lines, but broken gray lines, for they indicate a rural road. Down the list, symbols for campgrounds and green background suggest forests; jagged, black outlines, the continental divide with elevations listed at 10,250 feet and 12,347 feet; and wandering blue lines declaring rivers too.

Our internal compass and sense of the winds proved to be correct when we migrated. We've been in the Elk River Valley for over forty years. Our children often say they couldn't have imagined a better childhood, one in which they learned self-sufficiency, the importance of dependability, hard work, and cooperation.

When I reflect on migration and survival of the next generation, I remember watching our dog, Griz, return home after a hike on the hill. Once home, I spot hitchhikers in his fur. We call them porcupine eggs—small, tough, flat oval seeds from the monkshood plant, also known as queen of poisons or blue rocket. The blue-purple flowering plant belongs to the family *Ranunculaceae* and spreads free-wheeling across the lower hillside. Thanks to Griz, a symbiotic traveling companion, the seed pods migrated that afternoon on Griz's coat, enhancing their survival as the next generation of the monkshood plant through distribution.

Have we not followed a similar path to all natural life? A knowing, a yearning, a desire to seek, survive, and carry on for the next generation. Our children in recent years each migrated back to home ground after being away for a number of years. Our son, Andy, and his family live nearby. At our barn he trains quarter horses for competition. Cassidy, our daughter, lives on the ranch with her husband, raising their son and daughter in the same traditions with which they grew up.

While the valley has provided sustenance and shelter, it also presents us with ongoing challenges of managing the land, the water, and the future of this place. Can the ranch be sustained for the next generation? Will our grandchildren have the same reply our children did?

The river wanes this August. Land is limited. We search for innovative ways to support the ranch for our son and daughter and their families. Capacity for additional profit-producing animals is limited. Drought sucks life out of the meadows and draws; cattle head home from grazing on the hills, desperate for water; and fish habitats downstream require a call on the river to give them hope for survival.

Yet, I know, too, the shade of the aspen and cottonwoods, decades in the making, will continue to provide a retreat at our home place. In spring, the river still rises as though to say, "Believe." Elk Mountain, Hahn's Peak, and Sand Mountain stand as sentries in my mind, eternal messengers of time. Perhaps the earth is everlasting. Just last night, the sandhill cranes practiced their gathering on the Lower Elk—their annual migration from the high country back to the Rio Grande, waiting nature's notice for departure.

We are home. We will not gather to take our leave for a winter home ground. But, we wonder, now that our son is here, our daughter hoping to settle here as well, can this ground carry them as well, provide shelter and sustenance in the face of an uncertain future. Or will they and we, too, begin to look for a map of new land, noting our legends, listening to hear a notice that we all should depart?

RANCH LIFE

SIX

A Scaffold

L AST SEPTEMBER, I NOTICED A FEW TAN PINE CONES IN MY flower pots on the back deck. I wondered if they'd dropped from the limbs of two nearby spruce trees. But they were arranged beneath the fading fern and pansies, as though stowed on purpose. I checked again a couple days later and found the stashes had grown, nearly overflowing the ceramic rims of each pot. I was soon suspicious of a new resident to the ranch.

Over the last several years, we've seen new animal life—some passing through, others settling in. The list is short to date but includes antelope, European pine marten, the golden eagle, and the gray squirrel. We see the migratory antelope wander in and out of the spring meadows and again come fall. One spring morning a few years ago, a marten peeked out from behind a cottonwood as I watched from the kitchen sink. He'd spied a small sparrow's nest in an old wooden bird house hanging from the tree. The golden eagle nested here this summer south of the house in the cottonwoods, its raptor wail captivating enough to put a pause in my day. Later we followed the eaglet's maiden voyages to the thermals on the hill. And now I watch the daily comings and goings of my suspect, the gray squirrel.

Gray squirrels have been known to gather up to ten thousand pine cones in a season. As they gather, they hide their bounty in small caches. Our resident gray squirrels are scatter hoarders while others, often deep in the woods, are larder hoarders, stashing pine cones, acorns, berries, insects, and seeds in large mounds mixed with forest debris called middens.

My suspect scattered his stash until he could take it to a safe place near his drey, a nest built from sticks and leaves and wrapped with long strands of grass. It was a temporary arrangement, part sleight of hand, part energy-saving device to get the most gathering done on any given day. Within a week of my initial sighting of the small cones, they had disappeared.

Even though the gunmetal-gray runner on the rail is a rodent, I find myself watching him with delight as he travels along the top fence rail, safe from most prey except the eagle and hawk. His superhighway takes him from pine tree to pine tree as he scavenges for pine cones, returning home to his drey in the cottonwoods. In my observations, I've concluded his daily work is predictable, his work ethic industrious, his commute firmly established.

I admire the rail runner. His routine accomplishes what Nicole Walker writes of in "Of Constancy": "A well-worn routine is a life capable of heavy lifting." The gray squirrel ensures his survival by the lifting of a winter's worth of pine cones, carried in stages—from loose cones to sequestered cones to cones finally safe in the cache of his drey.

Walker's observation follows me throughout my days. It follows Pete too. The seasonal routines secure a scaffold for the heavy lifting of our ranch work. Most years, it sets in motion in May after the meadows give up their wet fleece. The first chores insist on attention, a clearing away of the deep winter so summer may unfold. Pete and I both begin with chores to reorder our landscapes, awaken the earth, and open waterways. Each day it's as though we breathe life into preparations for the summer solstice. The first task to call out to Pete is the restoration of the fence lines. He and his hired hand load up the ATV with wire, fence stretchers, staples, and tough work gloves to fix broken fence lines that succumb to winter's deep snows. Once the fence is secure, livestock can be moved in for grazing and horses are safe in their home meadows.

Next, the John Deere fires up and the meadows are brought to life by harrowing—a deep raking, disturbing the earth and grass. Once the harrow tines release the hold of old meadow growth, May's light washes over the smallest of young grass shoots; once the harrow tines pierce the hard earth, it accepts nitrogen and rain.

And finally, Pete hooks up the ditcher to the John Deere PTO (power take-off) and heads out to the irrigation ditches. It's there he drags through the waterways, through old remnants of timothy, brome, and slew, clearing the artery, the lifeline soon filled with icy waters.

I follow Pete but into parcels of land, soil, and water of a different kind. The raspberry patch, like the fence lines for Pete, call out to me before the snow on the north side of the aspens takes its leave. I prune with an insistence. Until I order the scraggly patch, I'm unsettled each time I look at it from my kitchen window. It must be done: the raspberries, the responsibility, the giving and the receiving.

After the homestead rhubarb plant erupts, but hasn't unfolded, I pull the tiller from the machine shed. Like a dear friend I hadn't seen for a year, it so willingly fires and tills the gardens with me at the helm. Once I turn it off and drag it up over the last raised bed and return it to the shed, I see a fine and moist soil unearthed, reborn.

Then I prepare for that icy water coming down Pete's clear waterways. I roll out the hose carts from storage. One for the house, one for the arena, one for the bunkhouse. I twist the ends onto a black line from the pump in the garden ditch hidden away in the aspens and hawthorns. When lawns warm and the seeds of the yellow bean, the eye root of the Yukon Gold, and the Hearty Girl tomato plant settle in that fine soil, I'll be ready to water.

I, like Pete, find life eases a bit when worries over the meadows, fence, and waterways—and for me, the pruning, tilling, and watering logistics—subside. For all the work that follows simply reels out from our preparations.

The sequential chores, the repetition of ranch necessities has a way of quieting my mind, lifting the weight I carry as I age. I have yet to conclude what exactly is ahead of me. What exactly is it that explains our existence here and our death beyond the physical world? Where exactly did death take my mother and my grandmother? In the tasks of the ranch, in taking control of my day and daily living, I find the questions ease in the rhythm and the beat of routine.

On these days, I feel fortunate, for I know that ease is not always guaranteed. On occasion, when we're engaged in daily and seasonal chores, I find the labor of the routine weighs rather than lifts up. When a seasonal task is complete—whether I weed a garden or rake the hay meadow—my efforts feel acutely temporary. The weeds grow back, the horses will consume the hay, and then Pete and I will hay all over again next summer. Rather than comfort in the hollow of the repetition, I hear echoes of existential angst.

As a young adult, I often visited my maternal grandparents in Cheyenne, Wyoming. When I arrived, my grandfather, dressed in a V-neck cardigan, dress shirt, and slacks, opened the metal screen door before I stepped onto the front steps. His hug seemed to say, "You're all that matters this afternoon."

With the start of each day, he shares Bible verses and a breakfast of tea, poached egg, and dry toast with my grandmother in their modest 1930s home. He reads the *Denver Post*, the *Wyoming Tribune Eagle*, and the *Rocky Mountain News*. With a simple fold to each one, he stacks them up and places them next to his easy chair. Midmorning and again in the afternoon, he puts on his black fedora hat and walks a mile. With purpose he carries down neighborhood streets, stopping to say hello to anyone he meets. On a summer day or perhaps when the winter lingers too long, he extends his outing to Holliday Park, circling the lake where his eldest son lost his life at thirteen.

In the kitchen, my grandmother wears a calico bib apron, a kitchen towel in her hand ready for the roast chicken, her light rolls, and simmering bacon and green beans. In the cupboard, she's layered her crisp sugar cookies with wax paper and carefully placed them in a tin. Earlier, she set an extra leaf in the small dining room table, covered it with white linen, set her mother's silver and porcelain rose plates for dinner.

Later, we clear the table, my grandmother fills the sink, and my grandfather and I grab a fresh kitchen towel. We visit, we laugh, we put dinner away. I hang my kitchen towel to dry on a hook near the wall phone where a Union Pacific calendar always hung. It was there I remember my grandmother hearing her younger sister say of their older sister, "Betsy's gone." It's there I'm told my grandmother, on the evening of her oldest son's death, also heard word from her Iowa farm that her beloved father was gone.

Several years ago, I came across a Buddhist quote: "It doesn't matter what you do, it matters how you do it." When I recall the wisdom, I consciously slow down and watch the task at hand: an extra glance at a weed hidden in the foliage of a peony, a more careful turn of the rake or the harrow to cover all the ground I pass over, or a deeper thought to my watering with the drought in mind. Giving my full attention in creating order in my world offers a quiet reassurance, the temporal nature of the activity receding into the background of those moments.

This Buddhist wisdom reflects the kind of refuge I knew whenever I visited my grandmother and grandfather. In the memory of my grandfather walking out of the door of 2012 Duff Avenue for his daily walks, and my grandmother pulling the plug from the kitchen sink after the last pot was dried and saying to me with a quiet laugh and smile: "If only life weren't so daily;" I sense, even though life weighed and at times crushed, my grandparents demonstrated a faith in the value and purpose in a measured and purposeful daily life—even in moments when routine perhaps tugged and weighed on their hearts.

SEVEN

THE HEM OF THE LAND

WHEN THE LAST VESTIGES OF WINTER RECEDE ON our ranch, the fence lines sag, weighted all winter by snow stacked deep and piled high across the wires. The season's load pulls staples out, splits wire, and occasionally, snaps off fence posts where they disappear into the soil.

Fixing fence in the spring is critical. In Colorado, property owners are responsible for fencing out livestock of adjoining landowners and fencing in their own. For ranchers like Pete, secure borders keep our livestock and horses where they belong—safe and home. So come spring, he eagerly awaits restoring the lines.

Each morning, from mid-May to mid-June, he walks out the door dressed in a wool vest and long sleeve shirt, worn wranglers and his working cowboy boots. Out in the machine shed, he packs up the John Deere Gator with a roll of barbed wire, fence stretchers, staples, a good hammer, and extra posts, often recycled from other ranch projects. He also takes a chainsaw to clear sagebrush along the fence line.

For Pete and every rancher, handling and managing the double-stranded wire requires strength and patience. The heavy wire, punctuated intermittently with sharp twisted two-point wire knots, is difficult to twist and turn. So, while essential, it's often a maddening tool with which to work. Pete's pace at first is brisk, but the tedium and difficulty of splicing and twisting wire for a repair slips in as the day wears on.

Over the years, building and maintaining boundary fences echoes the early West. The story of the development of these borders is well told by Laurie Winn Carlson in her book, *Cattle: An Informal*

Social History. In the mid-1800s, the western plains, grazed largely by great bison herds, supported many native tribes, including the Crow, Blackfeet, Cheyenne, Comanche, and Arapaho. However, with westward exploration and settlement, the herds faced near extinction by the end of the nineteenth century. The railroads' builders sought to thin them, believing they were a threat to their locomotives. Back East, a burgeoning shoe industry created a high demand for bison hides. Commercial hunting supplied fur and hides for prized robes and rugs. And the introduction of bovine diseases from domestic cattle posed deadly consequences.

After the systematic extermination of the plains buffalo and the forced government dislocation of indigenous tribes, the prairie and grasslands were left ungrazed. A surge of interest in Western lands by Americans, English, and Scots for raising livestock soon led to overstocked ranges, forcing individual settlers to establish boundaries to protect their land, crops, and small livestock herds with physical barriers. They used what was at hand to set the edge, the rim of their land. The Osage orange tree, its lance-shaped leaves and short, stout thorns provided a sharp defense; the spiny, prickly pear; the hardy, thorny mesquite; and the barbed wild rose took root depending on the western locale.

Unfortunately, the open ranges of the prairies and southwest soon became a landscape awash in disputes, including grazing rights, cattle ownership, and water rights. Range wars, often violent, transpired during the late nineteenth and early twentieth centuries in the American West. So the settler's thorny and prickly hem of the land turned to barbed wire. As a tool, it became an enforcer, a rancher's right-hand man. Fence lines protected their land and livestock, controlled the breeding genetics of a rancher's livestock, and prevented the spread of diseases found in free roaming cattle.

In this way, fence laws intended to create a civilized coexistence; and the physical boundaries between landowners left each to manage their livestock and land as they wished without dispute. In the spirit of Robert Frost's "Mending Wall," "Good fences make good neighbors." We've come to know this to be true, but only in the hands of those who believe individual rights carry with them individual responsibilities and mutual respect. When the repair of fence lines in the spring is shared, the ideal is carried out.

But there exists a resistance to a respectful coexistence in some neighbors at the edges of our land. Our fence lines adjoin five other private landowners. From time to time, neighbors cooperate in the upkeep and expense of the property lines. But most often it's Pete who needs the perimeter secure, not only to keep neighboring livestock out but also, out of courtesy to our neighbors, to keep our livestock in. Over the years, with a few exceptions, Pete is the one who repairs the adjoining boundary lines without any assistance from neighboring landowners.

When I've viewed our valley from the vantage point of a nearby hillside during the winter, the demarcations of private property laid down by fence lines are clear. Within each barbed-wire and fence-post frame, a clear spirit of independence exists. Of those I know well, most are devoted to a rural ethic of caring as though the vessel of independence—the individual rights to live as they wish—is balanced with a responsibility to others. But for some, the ethic of independence fails to hold a balance in the communal relationship of our rural neighborhood, fails to repair the mutual hem of one another's land.

So when the fences are fully restored in the spring, Pete breathes a sigh of relief. After wrestling with barbed wire and neighbor, the sight of a sure fence line brings a deep satisfaction. It is not without surprise after the completion of this ranch chore, without fanfare, he'll notice a shift in the landscape, as though someone opened the door and summer ambled in. In the distance, he'll watch our red Angus cattle in the evening before dinner, safe, secure, and grazing on our summer pastures.

EIGHT

A Crooked and Gnarly Wood

I WANT TO WRITE ABOUT THE WEATHER. I MEAN I WANT TO write about climate change. But finding the words and naming the issue feels fearful to the point of unmentionable, like when we avoid speaking of the dead and instead talk about passing on. "She passed away." "He's at peace." "She's in heaven." But never straight ahead. "She's dead." "She died."

I'm expecting my first grandchild in several months. In his or her lifetime, will he or she see what I saw today on the ranch where I live? The lone coyote who slunk across the meadow coming up from the riverbank as I sipped my morning coffee. A mallard duck pair searching for nesting ground as they wandered the cottonwoods outside my kitchen window. Three crows harassing one another for a mate and twigs for a nest, their decisions thoughtful but quick. The five petite white-tailed deer who ran across the county road, leaped over the barbed-wire fence and scampered south into an early spring wind. And the ritual first sighting of the diminutive rocky mountain bluebell and the delicate yellow glacial lily, faithful along my walking trail.

I couldn't watch Alfred Hitchcock and other scary shows when I was a child. The threat felt all too close and too real in my mind. And now in my sixties, when I lay in bed in the middle of the night thinking about climate change, I feel the same way: it's too close and too real. I foresee heat so high life must be lived inside; I imagine drought that threatens food stores and fuels fights over caches of seeds; I draw up floods in my mind more primal in their will each spring as though Noah's story may become mine.

I am powerless in the inky silence. I grasp for control to protect my children and grandchildren. In the morning, I ask in daylight, "how close, how real, how threatening?"

When my children were young, the micro-climate of our home was different. The year my daughter, Cassidy, was born, warm weather and shorts for Memorial Day picnics were never a given. The last few years, late May might be rainy, but short-sleeve shirts are hanging in Pete's closet. For over thirty years, Pete's hay season began in late July and lasted through the county fair in mid-August. This year he rolled out the mower, rake, and baler and made tracks with his John Deere in early July. In the eighties, I expected the tomatoes in the garden to freeze by Labor Day. As the gardening season came to a close last year in mid-September, I gathered green tomatoes from my vines and put them in the windowsill to ripen.

And in 2012, snowfall records were broken. We knew the run-off would be high, but when warm days and moderate temperatures at night collided, the melt accelerated. With my son, Andy, I stood on the county bridge over the waterway. Above the roar, I said, "Andy, my mind tells me we're safe, but I don't feel like we are. I've never seen a river like this. No one could survive in there." In the years since, I have failed to find the words for the raw power of the waterway that midnight. But if there were a nightmare, it was but a few feet below where we stood. The *Steamboat Pilot*, our local paper, wrote the next day, "Elk River sets a record at 8,250 cubic feet per second." Later, it was declared a 500-year flood event.

Thoughts and conversations about the weather, once light and inconsequential, a point of easy common ground in social conversation, now carry a heavier weight. Extreme weather events, like the 2012 flood and the changes in our seasons, shadow our thoughts about the future. Several years ago, I was reassured that mankind could cooperate successfully with the will of the earth when scientists believed the stratospheric ozone layer could right itself if human activity changed: less carbon emissions and less deforestation. Now, new predictions, statistical data, and forecasting models create a new disquiet and questions arise.

What mood are the climatologists in? Like me, do they toss in their fears, too, just as vulnerable in the silence of the night? Is there hope in the models, even those on the fast track? Will spring always erupt in the brilliance of green or will it one day weep?

Michael Mann, a Pennsylvania State University climatologist, reports that changes in parameters like temperature, sea levels, and carbon emissions have occurred ahead of the best projections. Global temperatures have risen in each of the last three consecutive years. Both the North and South Pacific regions have experienced one of their strongest cyclones every in the last year and a half. Tropical cyclone expert Dr. Phil Klotzbach reported that, on May 5, 2017, tropical storm Donna was the strongest May cyclone on record for the entire southern hemisphere.[13]

And the Western Antarctic Ice Sheet is on the brink of collapse, which in turn would destroy the ice shelf, creating a rise in sea level of ten to twelve feet. This would be catastrophic for coastal life in Australia and New Zealand. When our overheated Earth, now a greenhouse with only modest ventilation, threatens all living things with heat waves five times more likely to occur and floods from collapsing ice sheets, what would help create change?

The Fourth National Climate Assessment in 2018 reported the future of our world is truly threatened by climate change and a shift to more extreme weather events. Produced by thirteen federal agencies, the scientific report predicts dire consequences for health, global food stores, economics, infrastructure, and mental health.

I recently discovered the word krummholz in Barry Lopez's book, *Home Ground: Language for an American Landscape*. Krummholz— crooked, gnarly wood—lives in the transition zone between sub-alpine and treeless tundra, pressed by extreme vagaries of weather and physical circumstance. It survives at its environmental limit, its growth slow and irregular, windward branches failing to develop, but it remains a survivor, an elfin tree seeking low lying growth and intertwining to fortify and strengthen its hold. I weighed the question: as the extreme vagaries of weather create untold circumstances for mankind, can we maintain survival at some future environmental limit?

Laurence Gonzales, writing in *Deep Survival: Who Lives, Dies, and Why*, explores, with the help of science and story, how and why certain individuals survive, whether in the wilderness or in facing any of life's challenges. Those who survive do so by keeping their wits about them and seeing the world—the situation at hand—as it is. They don't protest the situation. They work with the reality of their condition, their plight, the scene as it is, one in which they need to survive.

Mann believes there is hope if we look at history. When we do, science and honesty prevail. When society delayed acting on issues of tobacco, ozone depletion, and the banning of chlorofluorocarbons, and lives were lost and damaged, we did eventually take appropriate action. So I look for hope.

After the signing of the Paris Agreement under the United Nations Framework Convention on Climate Change in 2015 by 195 countries, Norway agreed to ban all sales of gas- and diesel-powered cars by 2035, and France pledged to eliminate coal in the production of electricity after 2022. In addition, the Dutch government set a goal of reducing greenhouse gas emissions by 49 percent by 2030.

According to recent reporting from *National Geographic*, China is focusing on renewables: wind, solar, and hydropower. Germany currently generates 27 percent of their electricity from renewables driven by their commitment to reduce nuclear energy use. And with America's Clean Power Plan, the United States will reduce carbon dioxide emissions by 32 percent by 2030 and produce 30 percent more renewable energy.

In the middle of my nights, when I lay awake with restless climatologists, I wonder: if the largest contributors to carbon emissions do not take effective action, what can I do to tame rowdy rains and winds, and polar bears looking for safe passage over a dwindling ice cap? Will my small efforts to recycle and reduce my carbon footprint, along with larger renewable energy programs and clean air plans worldwide, be part of civilization's cooperative sculpting of a simplified but survivable existence, just like the intertwining of the crooked and gnarly krummholz wood?

The unanswerable. The unknown.

I'm reminded of the movie *Life Is Beautiful*. Set during World War II, it tells the story of a father and his young son's internment in a Nazi concentration camp. As the threat of death hovers each day, the young boy's father creates an illusion of their life, a sleight of hand in the movements of the small freedoms they both have. Guido, the father, tells his son, Giosuè, he must perform certain tasks, and with each task completed he will earn points towards a tank, a tank that would rescue them. As they lived each day, Guido was a joyful, magical mime for his son in the dysphoric scene.

While I don't wish to deny the reality of the changes in the climate, I feel the need to live with hope. So, as I place faith in science and technology to create a sustainable and viable transition zone, I will also be mindful to remember the inspiration of Guido, the joy in daily living the mime embraced so his young son would live each day free from worry and fear.

NINE

HISTORIC STEAM

A SOURCE OF STEADY STEAM IS ESSENTIAL TO THE ART of shaping cowboy hats. Many professional fitters use commercial steamers. But my son, Andy, well versed in the techniques of bending and drawing his hand over the brim and crown to achieve the perfect crease and fold of his cowboy hat, walks in the kitchen looking for a different source of steam.

After finishing up the June morning chores—feeding the mares and setting out a new round bale of hay for the geldings before another June day quickens and unravels—Andy and Pete stop by the house to shape their new summer straw cowboy hats.

Lean and fair-skinned, Andy turns from the open cupboard and asks, "Mom, don't you have a tea kettle?"

"No, I never use one anymore."

"But what about that one up there?" Pete asked.

The "one up there" is a nineteenth-century Finnish copper tea kettle, crafted with a dragon's-mouth flap spout and a hefty handle held in place by hand-cut flanges of copper and handmade rivets. I inherited the antique from my mother when she moved from her longtime home into assisted living.

As she often did, my eighty-nine-year-old mother, still bright-eyed and quick to smile, is visiting the ranch as a respite from her new home in assisted living several hours away. In years past, she arrived when Andy and Cassidy took their horses and livestock to our county fair in August. She'd been a loyal grandmother. So proud of her grandchildren, she would sit for hours under a hot August sun to see Andy's pig shows and Cassidy's horse shows. One of my favorite photos of her was taken at Andy's last fair. Standing side by side near the old livestock sheds, she and Andy smile wide, and in the scene, I sense the pleasure and comfort of belonging, one to the other.

After breakfast my mother sits on the kitchen bench seat with her walker nearby. It serves as a tray table if needed or a portable seat when turned around. When Andy and Pete walk in, she puts it aside and stands, eager to visit and watch their handiwork.

"Oh, yes, the copper kettle. You know, I never used it much, but that should do the trick."

My mother had always displayed the teapot on the antique German side table she dusted and polished every Saturday with a soft cloth and Pledge. As a child I imagined it museum art. But considering it up close this morning, I see an unglamorous, loyal workhorse, the old metal reminiscent of worn armor, the cool copper, heavy and thick.

Pete retrieves the aged teapot from the shelf and hands it to Andy. In his woody brown chore sweater, Andy fills the old workhorse halfway with water and sets it on the stove. The kitchen smells like breakfast when he begins: coffee, French toast, hints of syrup and fried butter in the air.

My mother spent some of her childhood on her grandfather's farm, wandering the Iowa hills and helping cook and assist the women serving the hay crews in the heat of July. So, with her fond memories close at hand, she immerses herself in the ranch, whether rounding up horses on the ATV or picking raspberries in the garden or this morning watching Andy and Pete's personal chore of shaping their cowboy hats.

For Andy and Pete, the right curve of the brim and the correct crease and folds of the crown are signs of personal preference and style. Brims may be flat, turned with just a fine lift or curled up round. The pinch of the crown varies, from parallel folds along the top, front to back, as though banks of a canal, or with a central squeeze in the front, referred to as a "pinchfront."

With the water boiling and the steam rising from the kettle's spout, Andy begins. Working one section at time, he holds the hat upside down with the brim over the steam. He moves the hat back and forth to soften the straw. Then with a firm yet deft touch he curls the brim with even pressure. Andy checks his work; the curl and curve set just right. The dexterity of his hands as they move without much thought, a cowboy's memory at work. Once the hat cools, he heats the next section of the brim.

Historians believe hats may have been the first article of clothing created and used by primitive man. Images in Egyptian, Chinese, and Greco-Roman art suggest that a hat was a mark of rank. The concept of a hat designed with a tall crown and wide brim, dates to thirteenth-century Mongolian horsemen. The crown provided insulation, the brim, shade.

The modern cowboy hat migrated from northern Mexico where the *vaqueros* ("cattle drivers") wore a hat with a wide brim for protection from the heat. What is known as the cowboy hat of today was designed and created by John Batterson Stetson in 1865. The Stetson hat and the American cowboy have long been wed.

While we watch Andy shape and steam from around the kitchen island, I ask my mother, "How did the kettle survive all these years?"

"I really don't know. It belonged to your father's Swedish family. Dad's grandmother, you know, Elizabeth, in Loveland, used it in her kitchen. I never knew what it really meant to him." Not knowing what my father thought and felt was not unusual. His heart and mind were most often a mystery.

Later, I discovered from my brother's genealogical work who carried the teapot to America. In the 1880s, the orange-red tarnished tea kettle was packed into a steamer trunk by my paternal great-grandparents—Beata Mattsdotter Ramus and Walfrid Julius Bjorkland—who lived in Finland, known then as Swedish Finland. (From the 1500s, all of Sweden and Finland were under Swedish control). Why they left Swedish Finland and how they traveled to the United States is unknown. Many Swedes who lived inland in the area between Vaasa and Turku on the Finnish southwest coast where my great-grandparents lived also emigrated to America.

Still sturdy, with just the fewest of dented hollows against its soft copper body, it remained valuable enough to family members never to leave behind. When it arrived in Loveland, I wondered, was it an artifact or a still useful tool linking the life and native country with the life they dreamed of living in a new land?

I recently read the essay, "Buffalo Eddy," by Scott Russell Sanders, in which he explores a history of a different kind in the petroglyphs at Buffalo Eddy in western Wyoming. There historians have documented Native American life among the American bison. When this period of their tribal life came to an end, Sanders speculates about the meaning of the remnants left when they abandoned their life at Buffalo Eddy: "When the orbit of their lives carried them away from the river, they could have summoned up those carved figures in memory, as talismans, as companions on their journeys. Just so, a man living long after the artisans left their marks may return to those figures, to that place, leaping thousands of miles, leaping centuries, as his mind seeks to gather meaning."[14]

What images would I have carved in stone? What artifacts would I have packed in my steamer trunk like Beata when she and Walfrid boarded the steamer bound for America, a world unknown? Like Andy's cowboy hat, a personal note of who he is and a useful tool for his daily life, what objects evoke a tie to or affirmation of who I was and who I became?

Whenever life required that I gather my belongings and move as a young adult, I packed my books. In college they fit well in two wooden fruit crates. And in the new, simple apartment, the containers became my shelves. Several titles remain in my library. Among those, *The Good Earth*, *Existentialism and Human Emotions*, and a copy of the revised standard version of the Bible that I was given at thirteen. The tie to memory so easily rises.

I remember the thirteen-year-old who loved the feel of her own Bible but struggled to understand where God resided. I settle in again next to the sixteen-year-old in the soil of Buck's lucid illumination of the cycles of life: loss and grief, hope and persistence. And I remain, just as the eighteen-year-old, both enthused and challenged by existentialism, the belief that life is our life to live with purpose, passion, and authenticity.

Not unlike the Native Americans' carved images and the emigrant artifacts, what meaning my books will have to those who discover them, I may never know. But they, like the petroglyphs, the tea kettle, and the message in Andy's personal styling of his hat—a future artifact—all leave ties to and clues about the journey of an individual, a clan, a long lineage of one's family, one's people.

How the tea kettle survived the many years of its utilitarian labor, moves from the Finnish coast to Colorado and many more in the intervening years of my parents' life together, I'll never know. I do imagine the voyage of the copper kettle, from Beata and Walfrid's hands to their great-great-great-grandchild, one of a fine, strong thread tying a knot between each of five succeeding generations, kept alive by loyal hands and desire for connection to family, and on this summer morning, kept alive as a grandmother bears witness to her grandchild.

Andy smooths the straw, considers the tip and curve of the brim, considers the crown with a purist's eye. Then he tries his hat on. How's the shape; how's the fit? As my mother follows the last of Andy's fine tuning, I envision the knot tying them together looped over a second time. The connection strengthened as the sun warms the kitchen, mid-morning light fills in, and my mother approves of his handiwork.

Once satisfied with the shaping of their hats, the creases and folds just so, the brims turned up to the perfect turn, Andy and Pete try them on and agree, "Just right, don't you think?" And my mother smiles, "Two handsome cowboys."

The day ahead of them, the ranch awaits their tending, they walk out the door, down the path to the barn, their hats now a mention of who they are.

TEN

In the Garden

MAY ARRIVES AND THERE'S A PULL TO THE DIRT MY imagination cannot ignore. I watch for the nurseries to fill up and the potting soil to arrive on pallets at my local hardware store. I scout hanging baskets and pots of flowers that catch my eye. I know in a small town they won't last long. So I gather them up and take them home to my greenhouse where they wait until nighttime temperatures warm and it's safe to move them outdoors. In this brief pause, I gather my tools, sort through pots, and open my garden shed.

Shovel

On the north side of the garage, my garden tools hang just under the eave, protected from the winter snows. For over thirty years, it's my shovel I first lean on for early season chores. Shorter than most, it fits my stature. With a sturdy wood handle and plastic red grip, its modest metal blade is the right size for my work: replanting and weeding in the perennial gardens around the house and tending the raised vegetable beds near my kitchen, just across from a small ranch stream.

With a sure press of my foot I turn up the sleepy soil, hearing the tiniest of abrasions as the blade rubs up against those few grains of sand in the topsoil. I smooth the raised bed for tidy furrows where I drop small Nantes carrot seeds between my fingers, then seeds of lettuce and spinach, peas and beans. I excavate for heirloom tomato plants—just six will fit the space—and seed potatoes—purple and Yukon gold. Later in June when the interlopers take hold, my shovel and I root out the sneaky bindweed, the prickly thistle, and deep-rooted grass.

I need not be anywhere else when I enter sleepy soil and smooth tidy furrows. The space within these four raised beds is without time, without shape, whole and unto itself. I am soul and spirit. I am an element in my own garden, not free and uncombined, but bonded to the sun and soil, shovel and seed, order and promise.

Pots

In October I stash my flowerpots—the plastic terracotta, antique fruit buckets, whiskey barrels, and large, lightweight self-watering pots—beneath a big blue tarp. Nested and stacked, they're stored for the winter where soon they'll be covered in three feet of snow. Once filled with spikes, ferns, vines, pansy, petunia, and portulaca, the vessels earned their rest, and I feel as though I have too. Come May each year though, we both go back to work.

As the sun warms and awakens, I gather my materials like a painter gathers watercolors. Traveling frequently through my favorite greenhouse, I hunt for texture, color, height, and bloom. When I walk in, Lisa, the manager, asks with a knowing smile, "So, what are you after today?" A lover of garden life, she's always interested in what it is I'm hoping to create.

Once I enter the embryonic space of the greenhouse, I scan for hues that catch not only my eye but stir something inside me with its warmth, intensity, or brilliance. I am lured, also, by colors that ask to nestle side by side; by texture—the rough, the ruffled, and the smooth—and by height—the tall and low lying. Each time I take with me just enough annual plants for a pot or two.

Every spring when I surrender to my gardening rituals, I follow my mother's tending of her iris and my father's tending of his roses. I also discover I pad along in very old footsteps. In ancient times, ornamental pots were often placed in established flower beds of formal gardens. I do the same.

The sizable self-watering pots, filled with a graceful grass, multi-colored celosia, lantana, pansies, phlox, and sweet potato vine, call attention to the potentilla under the kitchen window. Potentilla, from Latin *potēns*, meaning "powerful, potent." And indeed, they are.

Hardy enough to survive the harshest of winters, they are a staple in any landscaped garden in our high country. The terracotta and antique buckets potted with spikes and geraniums in red, pink, and white, also invite one to notice the columbine nod in sky blue and white beneath the old cottonwoods. Whiskey barrels, filled with red and yellow mums and marigolds, shout out near the August sedum in the west garden.

In Athens, flowerpots were also used to grow lettuce, wheat, fennel, and barley during the Festival of Adonis, an ever-youthful Greek figure who died young and was mourned by Aphrodite and later a cult of women. After the celebratory period, the women who tended the Garden of Adonis threw the pots into the ocean honoring his premature death and rebirth during the annual festival.

While I do not plant fast-growing edible crops in my pots, I do, after the riot of summer color comes to an end, throw away the spent plants and potting soil. The plants fertilize the aspen grove and the dirt settles in an old irrigation ditch where I return in the spring for extra fill soil.

In the sixth century, the Japanese discovered the Chinese art of *penjing*: the art of planting miniature landscapes with trees and plants, sometimes referred to as potted landscapes. The Japanese took up the tradition and belief that nature becomes truly beautiful when coerced into an ideal of beauty by man.

As rooted as I am in the natural world, I can only accept the Japanese belief in part. Nature is in sole possession of its own beauty. The intelligence that created it is beyond mine. But when I plant my pots in the spring, I search for beauty in each creation as I choose and gather plants for color, height, and texture.

In late May and early June, near my garden shed, I place the brilliant annual gems next to the pots waiting to be filled. With loamy soil and root starter, I begin by thinking about the placement of the pots. Will it be sun or shade, wind or quiet? Then the perspective—will it sit with one side exposed, or will it be seen from all sides? And then perusing the flowers I've gathered—what shall be tall and bold in the middle? Geranium, daisy, or fountain grass? What accompanies it best? Pansies, zinnias, or petunias? What loves a quiet, unassuming role? Fern, vinca, or sweet potato vine? For each pot, I repeat the questioning mantra. Searching for the answer, I listen to what pleases my eye, calms me inside, and yet feels balanced and whole in its complexity.

As I answer the question, the creation unfolds. With scoops of potting soil, an amenable host, not purely earth but containing perlite, old growth cedar, pungent peat moss and fertilizer, it nearly floats in my hands. I settle each plant in its spot, smooth the loam like an evening wrap around the crown of the lobelia, portulaca, and aster. And it's there I think I stumble across a personalized manifestation of beauty, practicing the old art of *penjing*: shaping beauty as though I know what it is.

Shed

A simple wood outbuilding, the shed has an allure all its own. First, the space is mine, one in which I store the tools and supplies of my summer labor apart from all other ranch tools and supplies. As the Old Teutonic/Anglo-Saxon roots suggest, a shed refers to separation or division.

Secondly, the garden shed is sided in redwood-stained cedar, my favorite color. Pete built it for me in 2004, careful to place it near the house but tucked in at the edge of the aspen grove, true to the old English shed, rooted in shade, shadow, and darkness. With rough lapped siding, a metal roof, and windows on the east and west sides, it's an inviting sight in June with window boxes potted with vinca vine and red and white petunias.

When the door, hung with wrought-iron hinges, finally swings shut in September, it means, with the close of the gardening season, my tools and supplies are protected from the coming winds, snow, and cold. Stored carefully in the left-front corner is my Stihl weed eater. It reliably trims the ragged edges of the garden beds, revealing the low-lying woods wort, snow-in-summer and moss pinks—all summer long. The shepherd hooks that held the conical moss planters this year filled with a delicate, cascading lime vine, rest against one another between two studs.

My solar-powered ceramic water feature, a deep ocean blue with a blowfish-shaped spout is nested under the potting bench for safekeeping. In an old wood nail cask, decorative garden stakes—the red and white cowgirl strumming her guitar and the pink and white flying pig—compete for space with green wire plant supports tangled like hangers.

In recent years, when I sort through the shed in September, I contemplate the day I can no longer manage the summer labor. I wonder, could the shed be a place of transformation? I entertain where a desk might fit. I imagine the summer light coming through the east and west windows, the shed door held open by a garden pot ablaze in geraniums, pansies, petunias, spiky ferns, and vinca vine. How would it be to rest in the shade of my garden shed as the daylight of my life shortens and turns to low light just as my tools and supplies have been held for safekeeping all these years?

In my reflection, I've discovered my garden tools possess what my soul may have already known. Residing within each one—my shovel, my pots, and my shed—are the essentials for life: work, beauty, and shelter. And so, it's not surprising to look back and see that "a pull to the dirt is one my imagination cannot and does not ignore."

ELEVEN

THE FACE OF LOSS

THE STORY IS OFTEN TOLD THAT FOR THOSE OF US WHO live and work or grow up around animal life, the lessons of life and death come naturally. For over thirty years, Pete and I have witnessed the deaths of family dogs and cats, cows, calves, foals, and mares. Over time, after the passing of Toby, Bernie, Casey, Bucky, Badger, Boogie, Brute, and Stan—our family dogs—and the loss of our ranch horses—Mighty, Angie, Dudley, Vegas, Daddy's Girl, and others—I've found death is familiar to me, but it hasn't yet come naturally to me.

Instead, when we lose an animal or a loved one, I find myself heading to the river where a small sandy beach invites one to enter the stream lined on both sides with dogwood and cottonwood. There, near the lap of the waterway, eager to be in its possession, I hope its determined current will take up my sorrow, might wash the pain of powerlessness and grief away.

Mighty Threat

In 1990 Pete purchased a young, racing-bred mare, Mighty Threat, a two-year old bay filly with built-in spirit and speed. We loved her diminutive but athletic build and the small half-moon marking on her forehead. Mighty gave birth to some of our favorite horses, like Jet, Threat, Vegas, and Allie.

Whenever Pete rode Mighty he knew he could count on two things: Mighty would buck at least once, and she would ride out with great heart regardless of the terrain or the task. Listening to Pete talk about Mighty was as though he spoke of a best friend, one of those rare best friends who comes along only now and then.

Approaching her late teens, Mighty easily foundered. When she did, her discomfort was apparent. As she wandered up the alley from grazing in the meadows, she stepped as though she were walking on hot coals. Foundering is a painful infection of the tissue that connects the coffin bone to the hoof wall. Horses develop it when they consume too much grain, graze on rich pastures, become overweight, or are overworked on hard surfaces.

Our horses founder because of our rich grass. So in the summer months we keep them off the meadows during the day and release them to graze overnight.

Mighty foundered more easily than others, partly a result of her age, and she couldn't even tolerate a night of grazing. So Pete confined her to a run—a small space with a shelter—and a feed of dry hay throughout the summer months.

The second summer Mighty foundered she was twenty-one. Her head hung low, her withers protruded, and her back drooped from age. Come morning and night when she was fed, she poked her head over the open Dutch door of the stall, waiting for someone to say hello, rub her head, or whisper something sweet to her. So, I did.

Horses are social, grazing creatures. Life in a stall and twenty-foot run, while necessary for her survival, acted as an arid substitute for her natural existence. I wished I could have taken her back to the house. I ached for Mighty. She was a sweet mare. And there she had to spend her days.

Late that summer, Pete awakens after midnight at the sound of a loud banging from the horse stalls. I hear it, too, and listen as Pete dresses quickly and runs downstairs to gather his boots, coat, and gloves. Once he reaches the stalls, he knows it's Mighty. In the throes of colic, she thrashes about, rolling from her side to her back and back again, her legs wild, flailing, slamming the shed walls.

Colic is painful and unforgiving. It refers to a range of intestinal distress, from a simple upset to a twisted gut when the intestines entwine. Pete knows Mighty faces the fight of her life, so he gets her up and walks her out of the stall into the arena about fifty yards away. Sometimes the act of being up and moving helps with colic. He also gives her a shot of Banamine, an anti-inflammatory pain reliever, to ease her distress.

Once in the arena, she lays back down and Pete sits on the ground beside her, stroking her side and hoping to comfort her in some way. He thinks about their twenty-one years together, her heart for the work and the spirit he knew so well in her buck. Her agony seemed so unfair.

But Pete understands these moments on the ranch. He knows when the time comes to "put down" a horse or calf or cow, the decision is an act of mercy. And it can come in two different ways: by a veterinarian who administers a drug that requires the remains to be buried four feet deep because it's so toxic to all life who might wander by to investigate—birds, whistle pigs, dogs, coyotes, and fox—or by a bullet. This night, in the middle of the night, watching a friend suffer, the choice, although difficult, is clear.

Pete knew Mighty wouldn't survive this colicky episode. She was beyond saving even with surgery, which is often unsuccessful anyway. Rather than prolong her suffering, he walks to the house to get his twenty-two. Back out at the arena he loads his rifle.

I had not gone out that night. I knew it was Mighty. And I knew if Pete wanted me to be with him, he would have quietly come in the bedroom door and said, "It's Mighty. I need a little help." But I know Pete, and in this circumstance, he needed to be with Mighty alone.

When Pete comes down for the breakfast the next morning, I wonder what toll the night had taken. "I don't know how you did that. She was your favorite horse. I understand why. I just don't think I could."

As so often happens on the ranch, Pete's reply to something he's forced to do but doesn't want to do has a familiar ring. "You do what you have to do. I couldn't watch her suffer. I wasn't gonna call a vet. She wasn't going to make it."

In the recounting, he sounds matter of fact. And he was that night. But he also carried the grief that accompanies the loss of a lifetime friend. And in the following days, I would hear stories about Mighty. "Anytime I rounded up cattle we'd be breaking through oak brush, down through the timber on the back side, and she never quit. You know she wasn't that big." Or with a laugh, he would reminisce about her habit of bucking when he first rode out down the road. "I was always ready. She had to make a statement and then off we'd go. I loved that mare."

Kitty

Kitty, now fifteen and a half, is losing weight and refusing to eat. Dr. Schwartz, a local vet, concerned about underlying issues of hyperthyroidism, suggests a few more diagnostic procedures, which may or may not be helpful. "But," he said, "I guess as veterinarians we keep looking for an answer that might prolong life."

I watch Kitty for several days like a mother holding vigil over a desperately ill child. My instinct tells me her tether to life remains tenuous. Ever hopeful though, I give her a prescribed appetite stimulant and encourage her to eat. I let her outside into her favorite world. Will a walk help her feel like herself again? Take away the pain? Against the evidence and logic, I hope the small adventure encourages her to survive.

Kitty's behavior changes abruptly overnight. She doesn't meet me at the bottom of the stairs when I come down for morning coffee. She hides under a side table, then tucks herself under a desk as her breathing labors, her meow desperate for help.

I meet the on-call veterinarian at the clinic, and as I do, I see Dr. Sam's fresh face change when she examines Kitty. "Her open mouth breathing is an attempt to survive. Her heart's beating like a race horse. Probably congestive heart failure."

She and the vet tech place Kitty in an oxygen box, a clear three-foot-by-three-foot Plexiglas container in which oxygen aids in her respiratory distress. Within minutes, Kitty relaxes, even stands up and begins to pace the sides of the box, a wild survivor hoping to escape the confinement.

As she revives, I'm tempted to believe she might survive. But I know the scene is delusional, and it adds to the pain of knowing what decision lay ahead. In a less than a minute, I ask the vet tech, "Please take her out."

I excuse myself and spend time alone in the quiet of the clinic lobby. On Sunday, a chapel of sorts: the silence and space an antidote to rushing thoughts of making a death decision for a creature I once thought would live forever. After all, she'd survived in a landscape of deep winters and predators. My linear mind knows the appropriate decision. My heart grieves. This is my Kitty, the mouser, the Kitty who loved her haunts in the cottonwoods, her retreats in the cedar-lined gardens, and her pleasure in winter hibernation.

I call Pete. I need to say the words out loud, to untangle, no not untangle, but to begin to braid my responsibility to end her suffering with the pain of ending a life. I know he understands the weight of the decision. The juxtaposition, the tenuous ground between wishing for life and ending a life never fails to startle me. I walk back into the emergency room, where I meet Dr. Sam in the hallway and look for her affirmation. She nods. The adult had come to "yes." My heart wrestles with protest but reluctantly follows along.

Dr. Sam inserts an IV wrapped in pink on Kitty's left front leg and says, "Take your time. When you're ready." Wrapped snug with towels in her open crate, I soothe her as she wiggles a bit as though still refusing death. My tears well again and again. I stroke her head and whisper, as I always had in the morning, "Pretty Kitty, my pretty Kitty." The necessity of befriending the moment when death takes hold and doesn't let go, left me helpless.

I motion Dr. Sam from her desk. "Are you ready?" I nod. With one dose to relax Kitty and a second to stop the heart, she was so compromised, she left the world in an instant. In a tender offering, the vet tech looks my way. "It may help to think of it as a gift. Kitty's free now." I drive Kitty home in her crate with the windows open, celebrating the Danish custom of letting the spirit of the dead free.

The northern Scandinavian countries have a deep, historical respect for and connection to their natural environment. Regardless of one's beliefs about life after death, opening a window for a loved one after he or she has died is a gesture of letting go. It is also a gesture of letting in, bringing in fresh air from the natural world; and in the simple act, one receives the promise of another day.

Mother

On an icy winter night deep in January, my sister and I return from dinner to our mother's room where she lay, we knew, near death. We sat close and read from her Bible. Her breathing is noisy or was it labored? I'm not sure. She lays quietly, comfortable thanks to hospice care. Within ten minutes or so of our return, she takes her last breath. My sister turns to me and asks, "Is she gone? Is that it?"

"Yes. She's gone . . . she's gone."

My sister had not ever seen anyone die. I knew in her question, oddly, that I was familiar with death in a way many others are not. I'd watched our animal friends, and I'd witnessed my mother-in-law take her last breath two years before.

I knew in my experience that the very act of witnessing and being present becomes a gift in the following days. The going out of the spirit is so clear. The physical body as it lays in the aftermath of the release is truly a shell, the housing of a being who no longer resides in their earthly home. This too, in a contradictory way, comforts. I see death. I know death. And in the experiential moment deep inside, my heart attests to the fact.

Father John, a Lutheran pastor, visited my mother each day the last week of her life. When he came to her bedside, he comforted with prayers out of a little leather book. His recitation was chant-like, as though one needn't know the words to feel its reassurance. I imagined my mother, unconscious, heard the care in his words. As I sat and listened, waves of grief washed over me. When Father John turned to leave, he offered, "Grief is love remembered, is it not?"

Looking back, the wound of mortality, the wound of losing a beloved mother or animal companion, is softened by the truth in Father John's question. I find relief in embracing my grief. When I do, I have an odd sensation that it is elevated. As it rises, I feel my heart lighten. And in the accompaniment of the knowing, being familiar with death, I'm encouraged to go on, looking to the periodic rise of memory as antidote.

TWELVE

Winter Slips In

WINTER SETTLES IN AMONG THE COTTONWOODS overnight, unbeknown to us as we lay curled, asleep in late October. The early gentle storm adorns our cottonwoods in crystals, frosts top rails, and lays a thin fleece over the meadows. Although tame, we know the silent shift marks the official turn of the season: the snow is here to stay, a premature seasonal point of no return.

As Pete and I huddle over hot oatmeal, looking out the kitchen window, I declare, "I'm glad I have to be at my desk today." He looks out, too, but in frustration bemoans the evidence: "I never quite get all the firewood cut when it comes early like this."

It's not that we're unaware of winter's approach. It does snow in October on our ranch in northwestern Colorado, but it often melts and recedes. Every now and then though, when the snow and cold settle in as they did last night, they remain, and the cover will be the first layer of the coming winter snowpack. We won't see clear meadows until spring.

As we look out, we fiddle to reset our seasonal logbook, knowing the uninvited change is here to stay. At least we knew what was ahead. We've wintered over in the valley for many years, and our knowledge, history, and experience serve as handy tutors for mentally preparing ourselves.

We brace for the moods of the chill. The low spirit of a deep cold, like an assault, freezes fingertips and toes and threatens to bring life on the ranch to a halt. When temperatures reach twenty and thirty below zero and Pete's diesel tractor won't turn over in the morning, feeding chores are delayed until the block heater warms the steel.

Every few days he'll clean ice from waterers near the barn and take an ax to the river where the cattle drink. If the horses and cattle aren't well hydrated, they might colic, developing a critical intestinal condition that may bring premature death.

We also prepare for winter's winds and heavy snows. They add to the labor, and we mentally prepare for the work. Every morning and evening, the horses—broodmares, geldings, and yearlings—and heifers must be fed. During any given winter, three to five hundred inches of snow may fall in the nearby high country, leaving three to four feet stacked up here on the ranch. For cars, trucks, and tractors to come and go, Pete bundles up in his Carharts and down jacket and climbs into the John Deere 6300 tractor with a large snow blower attached. In January he can spend half a day blowing out driveways, hay sheds, and barn yards. Then each and every gate, a half a dozen most days, must be cleared, either by hand or by the tractor blade, so the metal Powder River gates swing freely.

When I reflect on the fall season turning overnight, the forces and creatures in the natural world move to a beat often unheard and unseen. The turn catches me in the same way as the new fleece covering the meadows on those mornings late in October. The sweet purple crocus under the kitchen window so often erupts in April, already in full bloom above the lingering snowpack before they catch my eye.

Some years, when I spot the first sandhill cranes in May, they've already settled into the river bank and marsh, anonymous in gray. I'd missed their arrival. I hadn't witnessed their first spring flight up the valley. Then, before I knew it, the first avian clutches appeared. The sparrow, so secret, had already roosted atop the dryer vent outside my back door. What is it in their veiled eruption, their undercover return, their secretive appearance that catches me so? They slip into my world unannounced but so brilliant in their persistence and loyalty to the rhythms of the natural world.

Now in my sixties, beneath the surface the years have accumulated. For most of my life, like candle ice forming in October, the biological forces of aging were unseen and unheard. I had only an occasional reminder that the body can hurt, fail. I always recovered to an acceptable condition. But for me, there was a tipping point at sixty. And now I'm painfully aware of aging, and I'm angry. Like the intrusion of an early winter, who gave aging permission to steal my youth and settle in?

My body had always been dependable until the last few years when athletic injuries finally required surgery: knees, shoulders, and hands. My mind had always been dependable too, fast, agile, with a memory that could lock down a block of notes in a couple of moments of concentration. Now I struggle at times with what it was I was going to do next. It's a work in progress to create strategies for keeping in mind the next few things on my mind. Evidently, the glue connecting the neurons in my brain wasn't of archival quality. Why wasn't I warned I would be overtaken quietly in this way? What tutor could have convinced me of youth's illusion of immortality, seeing myself separate from an aging parent or friend, thinking to myself in my younger years, "That won't be me?"

Perhaps in watching my mother's later years, I came to believe it would be as she lived, as though there were no end. As I write, I know she believed that she was in some sense invincible, and as a Christian, if she weren't, it wouldn't matter anyway. Life was eternal. Life was to be lived to the fullest until the end, always with hope, always with gratitude.

But now in the aftermath of my mother's death, I find myself vulnerable, and I'm jolted into what James Hollis, writing in *What Matters Most: Living a More Considered Life*, refers to as a liminal state. *Limnos*, Greek for "threshold," a transition between two worlds. Just as my husband and I struggled to bring the new season into focus—the chill, low light, and daily demands—I feel the same disorientation, confused about identity and purpose, confused about what it is I am to do with the winter of my life.

The snow is mute, the slightest of breezes rustles the cottonwoods, and the mares huddle around their feeder. My husband and I wiggle in our jackets and hats a bit as we walk through the next few days. But as we always do, we turn and relinquish our resistance to winter's persistence. And it seems the turning into requires a certain flexibility of heart and mind.

After the opposition to the rhythm of the natural world, we embrace winter's silent arrival. Amidst the demands of the labor, we find winter's gifts if we choose, like the high spirit of a brisk day, the crunch beneath our boots lively as we walk to the meadows or barn, or the cheer of a Colorado sky blue overhead, or perhaps a warm February mid-day sun. When we see or feel the season's offerings, the chores, a project in the shop, or for me a snowshoe on the nearby hill, are not only unencumbered by the weather but enthused by the weather.

In my rebellion, which is surely grief in disguise over the quiet changes to my body and mind, I study my predicament just as Pete and I did that October morning looking out onto the undeniable arrival of winter, the meadows under cover, the mares huddled, and the wood supply insufficient. What choice do I have? I can't go back and reclaim the twenty-eight-year-old. I am indeed her at sixty-six, a grandmother, still active but not as strong as I once was nor as enthused about all the possibilities for my life. I search for that perspective that makes my world seem right, sensible, and acceptable. I am here. This is my life.

I conclude that my task as I age is the same task we faced over our hot oatmeal that morning when winter slipped in overnight. How will I choose to live amid the winter of my life? Change, whether perceptible or not, with or without our permission, comes with a persistence. It often presents challenges to our circumstances. It offers its gifts, too, if only we're aware, perceiving, and receiving the landscape in which we find ourselves.

On days when my heart and mind feel flexible, I sense a biological drive for life at work. Even though regret seeps in some days, I work at stepping over the threshold. I set goals for exercise and meaningful work, engagement with friends and family, and always nurture myself with healthy foods. In the labor, intent, and discipline of our daily lives on the ranch, I imagine we do the very same thing. In looking out our kitchen window when the winter arrives early, we have eventually discovered a drive to life by committing to our purpose here in sustaining the ranch, and with the commitment, our hearts and minds ease.

When I'm receptive and aware, I believe I hear in the biological drive a persistent call to life. On the other side of the rebellion is spirit at work not unlike the spirit driving the lows of the silent snow; the sparrow's hunt for foundling thread; the crane's liftoff from the Rio Grande; and the crocuses' rise from warming loam. I join the natural world—faithful to a natural beat and rhythm of an ever-changing and transient life.

FIELD NOTES

THIRTEEN

HEARTWOOD

WHEN THE DEMANDS OF THE RANCH SLOW COME autumn, Pete and I enjoy the peace of the open road. So, he picks the road atlas out of the woven basket by the stove and thumbs through the alphabet to the state that's been on his mind.

This fall we head out to California across western Colorado, the high deserts of Utah, the barren Mojave Desert, and finally into the San Joaquin Valley to visit our son in Exeter, California, where he worked as an assistant horse trainer. Filled with clementine and almond trees, grapes and avocados, it is also home to horses and gated, tree-lined estates.

Whenever we set out, settle into our seats and the rhythm of the road, I wonder: In the still and quiet of any view of a distant landscape from the capsule of an automobile, perhaps rock and desert, a granite divide covered in aspen and pine, what is it that soothes us, allows our unencumbered time to cleanse our minds? I have yet to answer the question, but I'm ever eager to surrender.

We stop first in Moab, Utah, where I attend the annual Confluence, a local reading and writing conference. I listen intently to Bill deBuys, conservationist and author of *The Walk*, who discusses the importance of pace and rhythm in writing, likening it to creating a musical lyric.

The following week we travel through Sequoia and Yosemite National Parks, and I find myself thinking about Bill's presentation, how words and their phrasing create music for the listening ear. Reading my way through park museums and their literature, I find words that sing out, both in their tone and definition: words like sapwood, heartwood, talus, Silver Apron, Ahwahnechee, chuckhars, and nunataks. I love the depth of what I heard in sapwood and heartwood, the light touch of talus and Silver Apron, and the playful beats in Ahwahnechee, chuckhars, and nunataks.

As a child, I found it difficult to listen to my mother read aloud to me. *A Secret Garden* was one of her favorite books. I do not remember the detail of the mysterious enclosure and the transformation of the little girl. I didn't know why it was so hard to listen. How I wish I would have heard the music playing in those words. I would have known more about what my mother thought important.

In Sequoia National Park, the world's tallest tree stands, nearly 400 feet high, its longevity attributed to its unusually thick bark and the layers of wood within, namely sapwood and heartwood. Sapwood is the youngest wood of the tree, drawing in and managing water reserves from the roots to the leaves of the tree. The heartwood, the innermost wood, is the oldest wood, particularly resistant to decay. Through the adversity of weather, fire, and insects, these layers of wood adapt, heal, and continue to grow for centuries.

Resilience. How can it be, a tree survives such wounds? I read the words and understand it in a way I should for a chapter test. Three stages: adapt, heal, grow. And then I recall Ernest Hemingway: "The world breaks everyone and afterward many are strong at the broken places. But those that will not break it kills."[15] I see the parallel: heartwood allows for the wounding, the breakage, and the repair. If it were so strong and steeled, perhaps not open to the wounding, it would fail to survive, as I might steel myself after a wounding, a loss, walling off my vulnerability, closing myself off to life.

In Yosemite's deep valley, talus is created when the tall granite wall's top surface layers slough off because of natural weather and mechanical erosion. A talus, in simple terms, is a rock pile. The talus provides nooks and crannies where native animals find physical protection year-round. Hiking to the precipice of Vernal Falls, we discovered the Silver Apron—once a rugged granite surface, now worn smooth over millions of years by the waters of the Merced River. The transparent and silken river flows over the Apron moments before it takes a thousand-foot tumble over a stunning granite cliff.

Nooks and crannies, transparency, and silken water. Earthly life, a paradox: protection and erosion, a soft hand of time and the relentless pounding of mechanics and weather.

In the recently renovated Yosemite Museum, I discover the history of the Ahwahnechee, the first native tribe to inhabit the valley. These early inhabitants called their home Yosemite, the valley of the gaping mouth. They subsisted largely on acorns stored in chuckhars, an oval storage bin made from natural materials, much like a bird's nest, and held up off the ground by a tripod of poles. When ready to use the acorns were ground into a flour the texture of cornmeal.

Crossing Tioga Pass to the east as we head home, a line of nunataks appear in the distance in sharp contrast to the smooth and rounded granite domes and walls of Yosemite Valley. Nunataks are rugged high mountain ridges standing high enough above the glacial fields to have escaped glacial erosion.

In the simple exercise of listening for the music in the words sapwood, heartwood, talus, Silver Apron, Ahwahnechee, chuckhars, and nunataks, my curiosity was captured. Now home in my reminisce, I wish I had known the same intimacy, the same capture as I sat next to my mother as she read aloud to me.

FOURTEEN

FREE TO WANDER

FOR ALL THE YEARS I WATCHED OUR CAT KITTY COME and go from the house to her woods, meadows, and river, I never feared for her, except on one occasion.

My husband and I worry as we sit down to dinner. Pete looks out the window to the south and notices two creatures walking carefully across the meadow. "Are those foxes or coyotes?"

Studying them I reply, "I don't know." The muted light of dusk made it hard to sort out the shape of the head and tail, defining characteristics between the two.

Pete grabs the binoculars and follows the two heading away from the river and turning north across our meadows. Most wildlife that comes to the river turns west to return, across the grassy fields, jumping the fence onto the county road and heading back up into the hills.

"Why are they headed north? What are they after?" I ask.

"Those are coyotes, healthy looking ones too. Wonder what they're doing around here in daylight. They've sure been thick at night."

Lying in bed we often hear the coyotes' chorus across the way. They yowl, yelp, and bark. Just as the cries of babies may communicate different needs, the coyotes reveal different intents in their chorus. The howl marks their territory; a yelp is a sign of play; and a bark is a parent's command to their offspring. Most nights I hear them staking out their territory.

After watching them trot on north, I say, "I hope they don't think Kitty's in the neighborhood. I think she's too smart, but I worry anyway." Coyotes are opportunistic predators, evasive and sly. I cling to the hope that Kitty's survived three years on the ranch for good reason—she knows the neighborhood. Knowing the rhythms of Kitty's life, a day later I thought the coyotes may have ambushed her. Usually traveling freely in and out of the house, she hadn't climbed the screen of the kitchen door to be let in.

Kitty came from a mean and wild barn litter. I hadn't particularly wanted a cat at the time, but mice were homesteading in our house. The son of a friend sealed the deal when he offered a mouser from his cat's latest litter. When I arrived to pick her up, Danny wore welding gloves to remove her from the kitten box.

I thought, *What have I adopted? An attack cat?*

When I brought her home, I named her Kitty. And at first, Kitty hid in the house. At the end of the second day, she warily walked down the stairs on a reconnaissance mission. We gave her a wide berth. Slowly she ate, meowed, asked to go out, and finally let a hand caress her soft coat.

Eventually, she insisted on being brushed before every meal, long and slow, over and over again. Some winter evenings she'd cuddle up close with me on the couch, every now and then on top of my crossword puzzle. Early in the morning she'd join me on the kitchen bench for an easy tummy rub, her eyes closed, purring as though she'd been transported to another world. And when she had enough of the intimate moments, she'd strike my hands with paws and claws as though I were a mouse and she meant to win. I'd quickly draw back and just as quickly she'd twist and roll from her back and leap to the floor. When I felt rejected, I tried to remember she was, for good reason, an able fighter.

Cat lovers often ask if I let Kitty out—a question that still surprises me. I believe cats are meant to be outside, roaming free. I identify with Kitty and all my pets. I wouldn't want to be confined, kept from exploring the world I live in. To do so would be like taking away my senses, to mute my existence.

A National Public Radio (NPR) writer once referred to the out-of-doors as the "daily newspaper for dogs."[16] I know the same is true for Kitty. She needs to know who or what has traveled through her haunts, the mood of the weather so she can decide where and when she will wander. And how fortunate she is to live in an open landscape where meadows nestle next to our home, cottonwoods line the river and shelter our daily living and paths for her clandestine wandering.

I wonder: isn't this what we humans do too? Make assessments and interpretations of the world we pass through—the people, the interactions, the problems and tasks to be fulfilled, sensing the elements that touch our skin and the inside of our nose, inviting us to enter in. Who would we be if we were held against our will from the landscape of our wanderings, investigations, and relationships?

So daily, in good weather, I open the kitchen door and she slips out into familiar scents: grass, earth, and wood. She might walk the fence, hunting for mice or voles, or rest safely in warm cedar mulch, hidden beneath the cotoneasters. Kitty also sits pretty on a large boulder in the shade of the old cottonwoods. I imagine her listening to the chickadees or on the lookout for the fox headed to its den under the old chicken house.

I became quite worried about her after Pete and I spotted the coyotes. She hadn't climbed on the screen door in twenty-four hours. So I looked for her when I walked to the barn and scouted for her in the nearby meadows. Was there evidence of a fight, a wounded Kitty, a bleeding Kitty, or even a dead Kitty? The predators could have won last night. Should I have held her captive in the house? What was I thinking? She had special powers over these sly neighborhood gangs. I tried to forget her absence. I stayed busy to avoid the "what ifs." But guilt settled in.

When Kitty came into my life, we were as tight as one human can ever be to a feline. Our intimate moments were of her choosing, but most often in the evenings when she could curl up next to me on the couch or first thing in the morning when she wanted pampering.

Then Emma, my Boston terrier, arrived and Kitty knew my allegiance had shifted and she made contact ever so briefly, showing little, if any protest. It was my fault. I had acquired Kitty as a mouser, not a best friend. But she lived in the house and I had offered companionship. When I chose Emma, I abandoned Kitty's wish for quiet time in my lap. Had I abandoned her again by not protecting her?

After putting clean towels away late the next afternoon, I wander down the stairs thinking about dinner. As though I'd stepped into another frame, there on the entryway rug, Kitty rolls playfully as though the neighborhood teen party happened to have lasted all night. When I arrive, I imagined she says, "What's the big deal, Mom? Geez, you worry too much."

At that moment, I remember the relief I felt when my teenage children arrived home when I'd been worried about where they were and what they'd been doing. As I discover her, Pete walks in from the mudroom kicking off his boots mid-stride. "I thought *you'd* be happy to see her."

"Where did she come from?"

"I don't know. She was waiting at the door when I came home. No signs of a fight. She's just too smart."

If there had been predators nearby, she'd outfoxed or perhaps, out-coyoted them. I so admired Kitty's resourcefulness, her ability to know where it's safe and where she risks her life. I considered her my street-smart homebody.

FIFTEEN

Surrender

EACH MORNING, AS NIGHT EASES INTO DAY, I PAD DOWN the stairs for coffee. But before I pour the light roast brew, I open the door for Grizzy Bear. Out he goes, first twirling and winding up like a discus thrower, then releasing into a sprint across the lawn to the fence. It's there he greets the mares. Then down the cottonwood trail to the barn, and with a turn he heads to circle the two ranch cabins.

I've interpreted this intense circling journey as an expression of his deep instinct to guard and protect. Going out into his territory, he makes an inventory of any change, then by his presence, secures the property for the new day. Once his home is safeguarded, Griz returns to the house and sits on the deck watching dawn rise.

One late winter morning after his scouting ritual, I spot Griz on the snow-covered lawn surrounded by two magpies. Even though their striking black and white plumage draws my eye, they annoy me. Often noisy and unfriendly, they dart from cottonwood to cottonwood. Known to aggressively drive off other species of birds, I anticipate they would be sassing Griz. Then I fully expect Griz to do some harassing of his own.

But the three creatures engage in their own quiet interaction. I'd never seen magpies act so congenial. The three seem to be friends. I want their low-key play to go on, but the magpies casually wander off, and as they did, Griz sniffs for more of their scent. I wonder what he learned about the two: were they male or female, young or old, what mood were they in?

That afternoon I take Griz and Emma snowshoeing. Approaching the top of a mature oak, sage, and chokecherry-covered hill, I hear a loud "Caw!" So loud, I suspect a coyote or fox might be very close up ahead.

Searching for the source of the sound, I soon realize it is from above; a large eagle calmly soars and repeats its "Caw!" Its tail and wing are accented in white, reminiscent of Native American designs.

Curious about the distinct pattern of white on the wing, I discovered later that this was a young golden eagle, prevalent in the western United States and still sacred to Native American people. Only Native Americans enrolled in a federally recognized tribe can collect eagle feathers for ceremonial use, often recognizing unusual leadership and bravery.

I soon recognize roots of the designation. The eagle is joined by two ravens, known for their acrobatic flying skills; and the threesome go at each other like military pilots practicing dogfight maneuvers: fast, sharp turns with the kind of energy it takes to kill. Quickly, it's apparent this practice session is just neighborhood play.

Then the golden eagle and one of the ravens, naturally adversaries, continue sailing on a small thermal, shadowing one another, at a military ease. The raven sails just above the eagle and then at its side, the eagle's dihedral wings taking full advantage of the wind's lift, allowing him to drift and float and rest. Around and around they soar, enjoying the relaxing moments after practicing their role as predators in their sky-built home above the hill.

I'm usually watchful and aware in my habitat. But these playful avians and Griz and his magpie friends made me pause. I had witnessed such unusual interspecies behavior between the ravens and the eagle, and the magpies and Griz. How much more would I see, how much more would I learn if I allowed the natural world to more frequently capture my eye? I know the invitation is standing.

The average brain weighs three pounds and is capable of infinite connections, utilizing one hundred billion neurons and ten thousand synapses each. According to the Laboratory of Neuro Imaging at the University of Southern California, the average person has about 48.6 thoughts per minute or seventy thousand thoughts per day. The Buddhists coined "monkey mind" to refer to our propensity to leap from one thought to the next in the ongoing internal chatter of our intellectual minds.

When I carry along in the landscape of my rural home, my mind is often in high gear, just as the scientists and Buddha attest. But deep in January, several years after I witnessed the magpies and Griz, I walked down our county road. There, after the frantic pace of Christmas, I found the peace a welcome denouement. With the winter air and low sun jousting—one sharp, one warm—my mind slowed, my breath eased. And then happenstance, a random meeting of things.

In the quiet up above on the oak-covered hill, a dark shape catches my eye. Without any thought, I sense a new addition to the neighborhood. As I stop to look closer, I see the finest of movements and realize the brown oval is alive. The discovery of a porcupine partially hidden in the brush captured me. In the moment of delight, I found a moving reminder to negotiate with my monkey mind: be still, be quiet, for in the surrender, the natural world comes to life.

In my daily journal that January, I made this note:

One might wonder, a bird's nest perhaps, thickening the shadows of that weathered brush. He sits high, a still life, his broad teeth peeling bark, his long claws shredding an old oak for bread. Hunched like an old man, he balances in twigs so thin, claws clamped, tail braced, safe in his coat of quills. I curl up to his winter secret as he murmurs and mumbles, gnaws and naps, all while hiding in clear view. No one sees up high from below on the dirt road. I hadn't until I stopped thinking one day as I wandered by.

SIXTEEN

INVISIBLE WAVES

third dimension: n., something that heightens the reality, vividness, or significance of a factual account, sequence of happenings, etc.

WALK THROUGH OUR RANCH BARNYARD AND HEAR CHATTER between Pete and Andy about horses in training and for sale. Through the air waves, barn names, nicknames ring out like Rocky, Romeo, and Ranger, Bullseye, Bossy, and Belle, Diva, Demi, and Annabelle. Later, perusing advertising from other Quarter Horse breeders, Andy continues at the kitchen island, "Listen to these, Mom. Walla Walla Wanda, Spoonfulofjam, Gunnatrashya, No Way in Hal, Im Hal on Heels, Dual Rey, and Miss Ella Ray. Aren't those great?"

These rich sounds take a magical path through my auditory canal to the tympanic membrane and on to the bony structures of the ossicles: the hammer, anvil, and stirrup. The reverberations then stimulate thousands of tiny hair cells in the cochlea. There, the waves and vibrations translate into electrical impulses perceived and interpreted by my brain as sound. At that moment, the musical evocation of the nicknames in the barnyard is brought to life.

I realize I often reflect on my experience in the physical landscape of the valley in which I live through sight—the visual evocation of my world. I'm reminded I must listen, too, for what I hear throughout my day. So I set out to explore the accompaniment and this is what I discovered.

The coffee pot sizzles, the timer clicks. The gas stove creaks as it heats, and my dog Emma lays curled, silent in her comfort. Silence is a sound, correct? The river rushes as all writers write, but what else does it do? It lolls, ripples, and roars in its own way. I hear a crow in the cottonwoods as though mad or impatient. And yesterday, I heard a crack and small crash in the brush on the hill bigger than a mouse or a vole. But who? What? My question left unanswered as I carried on along down the hill. Once back home, the machinery marked the afternoon: the start, choke, and puff of the John Deere; the rumble and high whine of the lawn mower.

The day filled in, layered like a visual artist strokes background, middle ground, and foreground onto the canvas. These invisible, insistent waves from the river, the crow, the choke and puff, the rumble and whine, so small yet so determined that we can't turn them back without covering our ears. And even then, they linger, muffled but headstrong.

My investigations stayed with me like a new insight, a treasure I did not want to relinquish. Shortly after, on a rare trip out of the country, my husband, two traveling companions, and I spent a day in Siena, a medieval town above the hilly Tuscan landscape of central Italy. As we toured, I carried with me an increased curiosity about the layering of sound in the physical world.

We were invited by an art tour guide to meet Antonello Palazzolo, professor of piano and exegesis of musical sources at the Rinaldo Francis High Institute of Musical Studies in Siena. Antonello has dedicated much of his professional life to the study of the origins of the piano and the first music written for it.

Guided to his studio through the cobblestone streets of Siena, we walk through an interior courtyard of a medieval palace, made of marble and stone. On the second floor, he greets us as the enthusiastic teacher—his passion for art and life brimming from his wide smile— lit by professorial gray hair, and energized by his trim frame.

His first question, "In art, what is the third dimension? It is essential." Antonello wasn't posing the question to confound us, he posed it out of his love for the essential nature of composing art, be it music, photography, visual art, or the written word.

With the sunlight sailing over the terrace and into a wide and long row of windows in Antonello's studio, we hear a mini didactic concert on an easy, warm April afternoon. As though they were his children, he plays five different pianos, each from a different period. As he plays, I listen for the third dimension, that which makes more vivid—from Latin *vividus*, "spirited, animated," from *vivus*, "lively, alive."

I conclude the answer to the question arises out of a

combination of the piano's unique qualities of sound and Antonello's interpretation of the music. The musical voice produced from each one so mellifluous, it layers and expands the space and time of the studio. Our senses fill with waves, vibrations, impulses—infused with Antonello's gifted hands—elevating us to a sphere we could not have reached on our own.

I carry Antonello's "third dimension" home with me. Whether it's the rhythmical alliteration of barnyard names, the grind of the John Deere, the wail of the raptor, the crash of elk in the oak, the chatter of chipmunks in the mugo pine, or my mother's last breath, sound layers my world. The invisible waves pressing on the timpani of my ear, pulling from the physical world a third dimension, an essential essence added to the visual world, making life more vivid, real, and true.

SEVENTEEN

HUNTIN' WOOLLY BEARS

hunt: v., to make a search or quest

EACH SEPTEMBER, WHEN SUMMER DAYS DRAW DOWN, when aspens turn saffron and rust, when woods crisp, and the air quickens, I love to look for woolly bear caterpillars crossing the road, right at the corner where cool cottonwood shade settles early in the afternoon.

Although based in folklore, my search for a predictive message from the woolly bear about the coming winter seems to serve a very practical purpose and a need to feel closer to the natural world. For those of us who live in this high mountain valley, if the natural world predicts a heavy winter, cattle will need more feed. I and my neighbors will need winter tires sooner and longer. And perhaps for some, the warning helps with the mental preparations of our landscape closing in. No one wants winter's chill too soon. Prolonged sub-zero temperatures and heavy snows push on our sense of vulnerability and fragility. We know how harsh the natural world can be.

This ritual is not the only one I follow. I join my neighbors in measuring the height of the skunk cabbage for the belief is, the height estimates the depth of the coming winter's snows. I listen for news of beaver dams, too, on the waning waterways. The higher number of damns, the harder the winter ahead. And then I eagerly hunt down the black-and orange-banded woolly bear.

Today, I find a woolly bear. They appear on the road in mid-September and early October. The hairy caterpillar is crossing the road in search of a burrow, either under a rock or in a decaying log, where it will spend the winter in its larval state. As I watch, the bitsy larvae looks fluffy, something to take home and care for, but for its protection, it wears a bristly coat. It sustains itself in freezing temperatures by producing its own antifreeze. Come spring, it transforms into the striking black and white tiger moth.

I watch its purposeful journey to a safe winter home, away from the hum of commuters. I wonder how it ambles with three sets of legs from its summer ground where clover, grass, and nettles have begun to die out. I wonder how it manages feeling its way with tiny eyes across the gritty resurfaced road. I slow down even more. The corner is blind. So small, I worry about its migration. I hope there won't be any more cars headed north.

Folklore tradition suggests that the wider the orange band on the woolly caterpillar, the harsher the winter ahead. When I ask Google, I discover that there isn't any scientific evidence to indicate there's any correlation between the band width and the severity of the winter ahead. The band width is a record of when the caterpillar was born. The wider the band, the earlier their birth in the spring which would indicate a shorter previous winter. The narrower the band, the later their birth in the spring indicating a longer prior winter.

When I hear the news, I am a child again, disappointed at hearing a myth dispelled. I wanted to believe I could depend on woolly bears, that they could speak to me about a world we share, but they know deep within. Just as the tooth fairy knew when I lost a tooth; just like Santa Claus knowing the desire of my heart. Woolly bears, tooth fairy, Santa Claus—myth, belief, surety—the world made intimate.

While I'm an inhabitant of the physical world, I feel a certain intimacy remains unavailable to me. And I keep coming back. I keep searching. Possibility endures in choosing to occupy an imaginative space emanating from the natural world.

When I hunt the woolly bears, I believe I'm looking to fill what James Hollis refers to as a personal and societal loss of myth: whether it's religious icons, indigenous stories, Greek sojourns, or wisdom from the natural world. With the absence of myth, he suggests we lose a sense of meaning for our lives.

Hollis defines myth as "an energy-charged image, or idea that has the power to move and direct the soul, hopefully in ways that link us more deeply to the mysteries of the cosmos, of nature, of relationship and of self."[17]

According to brain research, we humans, as we process sensory experiences, look for patterns and seek to make meaning out of those patterns. We're naturally wired to be curious and ask questions about the nature of this earthly life. In the attempt to answer, we may look to symbolism, spirituality, myth, prophecy, a link to the natural world, or some other source of wisdom that resonates with the patterns we seek to understand. The drive, the instinct for the hunt, the search, the quest is ingrained in our biological minds.

Though the woolly bear's power to predict the winter season is not absolute, as autumn slips into the arms of winter's embrace, I continue to hunt woolly caterpillars anyway. The ritual satisfies a deep need to know the physical place in which I live in a deeper way; seeking symbol and myth, I sense an enlargement of my experience, a greater personal celebration of all that exists.

Sacred Ground

EIGHTEEN

GATEWAYS

Gateway: n., any point that represents the beginning of a transition from one place or phase to another.

PETE AND I LIVE ON 530 ACRES OF RANCH LAND. IN OUR daily lives, we are aware of two landscapes: the open space as though seen from above; and the one we've internalized, the one defined by the smaller parcels of hay meadows, pastures and a nearby hillside. On most days, we carry out our lives within the borders and nuances of those defined sections of land, navigating our way through gates, wire fences, or in some cases, through an awareness of a subtle shift in the habitat understood only by one's quiet attention.

Gate: n., archaic, a path; way; North England and Scotland, habitual manner or way of acting.

Wandering through the barnyard mid-day in May, I hear Pete open the tractor door, "Hey, what are you doin'?"

"Not much, just finished tilling the garden."

"Could you help me? I've got to take this load to the burn pile. It's always easier if someone helps me with gates. Hop in."

After I climb up the John Deere and put one foot in the cab and one on the steps, we're off. The practice of standing on my perch is warned against in all tractor owner manuals. It's a tenuous one. With a tire the height of a small car at my side, one slip and I won't be of any help. But I don't mind the risk. The physical necessity to stay balanced appeals to a capable and youthful image of myself I cling to now that my children are grown.

First, we stop at the main gate, which leads to pastures, the river, and the burn pile. With a step from the cab, I unlatch the six-rail H&W metal gate, swing it wide and wait for Pete to pass. I return the guardian and hook the Kiwi latch, placing the thick metal hook, shaped like an open number nine, into stout staple secure in a tall wood post.

Leave the gate as you found it is well-known courtesy in rural areas around the world. Gates control access to water and feed, breeding, and protection of livestock. If the intent of the ranch owner is averted—an open gate closed or closed gate left open—livestock may go without water, cattle may wander, or a horse stallion may mistakenly breed mares.

Up the steps again and with a roll of the tires we head to the next two gates. Intersecting an alley where livestock and horses are herded to and from the barn, it's there I twice repeat my chore. Kiwi hook removed, the tall rail gate swung wide, Pete traveling through, gate swung closed, and the number-nine hook slipped back into the staple.

Sequestered below the barn in the willows and cottonwoods, the burn pile houses a pyramid of work history and a record of the seasons on the ranch. Pete's load in the spring is often made up of tattered winter remains: branches, clumps of abandoned hay, and old fence posts. A number of years ago, he hauled remnants of rough-sawn timber leftover from building a horse shed, painted barn red and trimmed in white. One year log ends were collected from the construction of the new ranch cabin we built on the footprint of an unsalvageable turn-of-the-century homestead house.

Remaining on my perch, I watch as Pete closes in on the edges of the refuse, lifting and extending the front-end loader high over the peak and slowly releasing his delivery. A tangled cascade slides out, each piece settling wherever gravity sees fit, as though pick-up sticks are dropped on a tabletop. With a shake of the front-end loader, the last of the waste reluctantly drops out.

Come late fall, when the life and color fades from my gardens, I, too, gather remains for the burn pile. I snip and cut, bend and snap the sedum, the lily, and the peony; trim the lilacs, cotoneasters, and loyal potentilla. When the potatoes and tomatoes, the green beans and onions have all been harvested, I pull the old, crisp tomato stalks, the green bean vines, and then round up the limp discarded potato foliage from the soil.

In the bucket of the John Deere, I layer the seedy remains, the branches, stalks, and stems until it can hold no more. I haul the load through the same six gates, often through the mud and muck of November's fitful weather. When I tip the bucket of the John Deere and slowly release my load, I regret the end of the season. I remember how the lupine's stout spire, peony's sweet lace, and lily's vulnerable furl each captured my heart through the season.

Near Thanksgiving, Pete will marry a match to fuel and torch the pyramid on a gray day, when the fire isn't a threat to life or the land. And with the fire and heat, what once lived; served a purpose; defined a perimeter; offered shade, beauty, and shelter from life's weight and work will be consumed.

Gap: n., from the old Norse "gata," meaning road or path, originally referred to the gap in the wall or fence, rather than a barrier.

When winter on the ranch settles into a more peaceful routine, I crawl through a gap in a metal fence behind the house for a brisk snowshoe with our dogs, Emma and Griz. No one knows what split the rails apart, leaving a hole in the middle like a bullseye. But it serves the purpose of keeping the horses in one of our winter pastures.

Emerging from the mouth of the gate, I enter the meadow where the bred mares feed, wander, and find protection in nearby aspens until their foals arrive. With their pasture next to the road, a few neighbors who pass by hold vigil all winter long. Some choose their favorite one to watch over. Perhaps Cali, from California, who wonders on a wintry day why she's here? And when the foals hit the ground in May, neighbors stop me on the road where I often walk, and I'm told, if they could, which one they would take home. The mares are in good hands.

As we cross the meadow, my heart speeds up, preparing to meet the demands of our snowshoe. For Emma and Griz, our walk is a hunt and perhaps for me too. At the far end of the meadow, I discover a scene of blood spatter on the snow. Searching for tufts from a struggle, I find a sprig of fur, more gray squirrel than vole. Perhaps an owl or hawk stalked its prey and with talons shaking snatched the victim from its burrow. As I search the remains, my imagination heightens. What was it like to be taken, consumed, with but a tuft of fur left as evidence of a life? I hope death came quickly.

Crossing over the county road to the service road leading to the summit of a small rise on the hillside, I listen for the susurrations of a world that knows time only in the arc of the sun, the wildlife guided by simple needs of food, water, and shelter. When I enter in, I begin to feel as though those needs are all I need too.

Emma leads the way while Griz follows behind me, ever the herding dog. I feel safer with him. With evidence of bear and lion on the hillside, I don't trust that my mini can of mace will save me if anything were to happen. It's the lion that concerns me most. They attack from the rear. Ever a feline though, they still fear the canines, making Griz a predator. I love that he cares for me in this way— without fail, loyal to my protection.

I don't mind breaking trail after last night's snowstorm. I feel hardy pioneering up the trail. So, as Emma and Griz search for scents, I watch for signs of life. With little on my mind but watching my footfall, I discover a Stellar jay's feather. I'd never seen one on the road. I claim it, draw my fingers over the vane, smooth the branches, and then tuck it in my zippered pocket.

Later I learn the jay's feathers molt completely over the course of a year, and the new pin feather erupts from the same follicle from which the old feather fledged. I also discover feathers vary for different purposes all in one bird. Eldon Greij, in *Bird Watching Daily*, explains, "Smaller contour feathers cover the body and leading edges of the wings. On the wings, the feathers help form the airfoil shape that is necessary for flight. On the body, they contribute color, which is important in courtship and for camouflage, and they form a sleek outer covering, providing an aerodynamic tear drop shape that assists flight."[18]

Without any signs of struggle—blood splatter, scattered footprints, or disturbed snow—I assume this feather followed a rhythm of use and desuetude, a testimony to a releasing of the old to make room for the new. I imagine the jay healthy, doing what jays do, its wings holding the small currents the way other avians' wings do, seeking a pure and simple pleasure above the hill.

Do I do what jays do, naturally release the old and then with a tip of my wing take up sure flight and pleasure on the hill? I wish I possessed the wisdom of the jay's biological mind. I struggle at times to listen to the susurrations of the old, the dispensable. Perhaps a distorted view of who I thought I was before I came into my adulthood: capable, not capable; worthy, not worthy; pursuing goals for proof. I believe the jay's biological mind would not have questioned what distortion to release.

Torii: n., from the first century, the Japanese gateway, most often found at the entrance to Shinto shrines; continues to symbolize the transition from the profane to the sacred

I'm slow breaking trail. The snow is heavy, filled with moisture. Emma comes back from around a bend to check on me. It's there she knows I never fail to turn and take in the first visible view of the valley. As I linger, a shift always occurs. I settle into the physical world of my tramp, a world I struggle to translate.

I first rest my eyes on the Elk River passing through the heart of the valley. I follow the cottonwoods until they turn east and disappear into Christina Canyon. I love the curve and meandering pace of the line. It slows my breath. Then I wander to Elk Mountain, a stout presence once referred to by the Utes as the Sleeping Giant. A local educator coined the inspiration for her students with the phrase "Awaken the Sleeping Giant Within." Each time I remember.

Finally, I settle into the whole of the lowland: its down-covered meadows and sparse settlement of homes, the thin etchings of barbed wire fences in the distance, the subtle pull of Long Gulch up its draw to Pilot's Knob, and then with a quiet return, I feel the plant of my feet in my snowshoes. Each time I recite the landmarks, I cross a threshold and the doors of a sanctuary open.

Shortly, I reassure Emma, "I'm a comin,' let's go."

Our destination is not always the summit. Today we finish at the top of what I call the "steep pitch," difficult to hike any time of the year. It requires a sure grip of my toes with each step into the snow. It's there, too, we stop and catch our breath. While Griz stands patiently at my feet, Emma is eager to turn toward home, but I beg her indulgence. The still and quiet hold me captive and won't let go.

At that moment, if it were possible to consume the silence, it would be as though I were drinking from a communion cup filled with the first icy waters to seep from the hills come spring. Every time I cross over, I return to possess the landscape in the same way I possessed my seat near the organ as a child in church every Sunday morning. Safe. Secure. Assured. After a few moments of peaceful breath, I no longer ignore Emma's beseeching terrier eyes. I agree to head home and tuck away for safe keeping the spirit I touch on the hill.

NINETEEN

WHITE SPACE

L AST SUMMER I LET THE MEADOW GRASSES INVADE MY perennial gardens. I failed to object to the trespass. The timothy and brome, thistle and bindweed filled in between potentilla, lupine, sand cherry, aster, sedum, and rudibeckia. As soon as the snows drew back this year, they greedily returned, as though they had a right, as though they'd proved-up their homestead. So when spring channeled her energy, I fought back. I took my shovel and hoe from their storage hooks and dug in.

I uproot the errant grasses and weeds in each bed. I smooth a fine layer of mulch between the perennials: the columbine, dianthus, salvia, and daisy. In a smaller bed near the kitchen window, I clear and till a space between the brilliant Oriental poppy and the delicate sway of the geranium. The reclaimed spaces murmur, "Take it easy. All is well with the world."

In the world of art and design, the eye rests when it settles on an empty space. Whether it's within the written word, visual art, or a garden bed, white space assists the viewer in taking note of what she may not otherwise see. I discover such a helpful example:

ceassiststheviewerintakingnoteofwhatshemaynototherwisesee . . .

It's easy to "see" that the opening, sometimes referred to as negative space, ironically provides clarity.

Within a larger landscape, I inventory the idea as I sit at my desk. Outside my office window, the wintering meadows, a smooth down coverlet, impose, insists on their space and their peace. Later I will watch foals in those meadows move out, away from their mothers, the distance between a space where independence and separate identity takes purchase. In the image, I remember my children at two, toddling away from me on the front lawn, pausing to look back for assurance, then carrying on with their risk taking and small adventure, creating the space between self and mother.

Reflecting on the peace in my gardens, I wondered, could I create other momentary retreats? In the litany of my to-do list? In my office? In my thoughts and my conversations? Could I uproot the obstructions to a more peaceful day?

I experiment with an overstuffed file of poetry. I sort and relinquish the poems that had served their purpose: first attempts, experiments, filled with the first language of a new poetry student. In the combing and winnowing, a soft light illuminates what remained. In my hands, the file of kept poems feels like a gift.

As I run errands in town, I remind myself to create the space to listen to others. When I pick up my dry cleaning, I ask the longtime manager how things are. With an understated smile, she says, "I just lost two gals, and we had the busiest week we've ever had. We still have fifty shirts and the locals' spring cleaning. But we'll get it done." Celeste never complains even in the intensified heat of July when the irons hiss and steam in the back room. Always steady, I admire Celeste's humility. She expects so little and gives so much.

My experience reminds me of the open spaces between the oak brushes on the nearby rise. For the elk and the deer, the lack of cover fails to protect them. In my pause with Celeste, the risk of the emptiness between us—to allow the moment to fill in and not bypass, not inquire—raises vulnerability; a protective shell collapses, and we are exposed. Yet, in that space, one breath, one pause, I stand in potent and fertile ground. The white space of social caesura, an invitation to connect self to other, an invitation to a sacred space.

At my next stop, I feel a pressing need to get home as I stand in a long line at the grocery store. There I am walling off the space of a simple pause: anxious, impatient, annoyed, mumbling the inconvenience. And then I remind myself of my research. Once conscious of the anxiety, I look down to a full grocery cart. The hammering in my heart slows. How many others in the world are never asked by a grocery store checker, "Did you find everything you needed?"

But will I continue? Will I pause?

My will may wane as interlopers of time—errands, noise, texts, breaking news—divert my attention from the peace in the paradoxical space of nothingness, my commitment eroded by the din of daily living. But as I consider it, this time of my life—one of slowing and assessing—calls me more and more insistently to the present moment.

With a growing intimacy with life's transient nature, the very thing I protest is now gratefully my tutor, prodding my return to present moments: my granddaughter's smile as she walks down the driveway by herself to greet me; the bale wagon picking up beautiful square hay bales for the barn, fifty at a time outside my office window; the cloud cover settling in over Long Gulch, portending a much needed night and day of rain; and the comfort of my Boston terrier, Emma, asleep nearby on my office couch.

TWENTY

THATCH

Whenever I'm asked to harrow, I climb into the John Deere and shut the back window and main door. The clank and rattle of the harrow, like an Arthurian King's chain mail with spikes, is more than I can listen to. Harrows, made from half-inch steel rods fashioned in the shape of diamonds with sharpened ends called teeth, do earthy work. I set my feet firmly on the floor of the cab and grab the wheel with both hands. The round and round of the harrowing route might look like a moving meditation, but raking wintered-over grounds, vole hills, and occasional clumps of old hay and manure makes for a bumpy ride.

Pete's harrow is a large affair. Approximately eight by eight, it's heavy and unwieldy. But its utility requires its weight, steel spikes, and strong but flexible diamond joints. Harrowing meadows in the spring stirs the ground, thatch, and manure, clearing the way for the coming light to warm the young grass. When a field is finished, how tidy it looks. The back and forth of the grating harrow rake leaves a pattern in the meadow as though shaded one way and not the next, reminiscent of fabric nap.

I, too, harrow my lawns, but with a smaller affair. I grab the four-wheeler and a customized harrow to stir up the lawns. The early spring ritual rattles the grass from its winter hibernation. Pete cut my three-by-four-foot harrow out of an old one, once six by eight feet. He secured two old tires on top for downward pressure, forcing the old brown grass to gather and scatter as the harrow passes by.

Today Emma and Griz join me. Emma in the front seat shakes from excitement and a chilly western breeze. Griz, always at the ready, settles into the bed of the four-wheeler. After just a few turns around the yard, the dead growth, rather than scattering, piles up thick and jams the harrow. Puzzling at first, I remember I overlooked the directions and fertilized a small area with a summer fertilizer last fall. The additional nitrogen increased production of root and stem tissues. The tool that usually eases my labor won't do. The thick thatch requires manual attention.

After I grab both the bow and leaf rakes from their hooks, I return to the overgrowth and draw back the old tangled grass, leaving open wounds in the lawn with each passing stroke. I think I'm digging in too deep; I need a lighter draw of my rake. The bare ground will never grow in. But I have no choice. I face the fact the grass is dead and must be taken out and, yes, only bare ground will remain.

With my mind settled, I continue working. I know the act of clearing out the dead growth allows for tender grass to begin anew. The careful raking prompts me to recall that death and new beginnings come with a regular rhythm in my gardens.

Along with harrowing in the spring, I prune back dead growth in the cone asters, sand hill Cherries, and Russian pea shrub. Their new growth mid-summer brightens the gardens around the house. I cut the raspberry canes back to two stalks and wait for the August harvest. Whenever I sort through the patch in May, the raspberries are robust.

Old growth and new beginnings come in my own life too. Several winter sweaters I'd favored for a long time come to mind, each once selected for the right weight, fit, and color. When I lay a hand over their weave, I say to myself: *you should find a new home for this one. Yes, but I don't want to,* I say to myself. And then often stack it back on the shelf according to its color: the blues with the blues, the reds with the reds, and the neutrals cozy together. In other moments, I'm able to relinquish the old, pass it along to Goodwill, just as I told my children to do when we prepared to buy clothes for school.

When my children left home, more old chapters cleared out for the new. I packed memorabilia, special clothing, maybe a stuffed animal and quilt into plastic tubs and stored them until they both had places of their own.

Each bedroom was transformed. Andy's, once papered in horseshoes and green, now sandstone and textured with paintings of aspen, birds, indigenous sculptures, and art. At my office desk, where Andy's bed once stood, I settled in to write.

Cassidy's room, once papered in cream, pink, and rose, now a guest room with horse prints on the far wall. We host family and friends there with views of the night sky and Elk Mountain down valley in the morning. How those guests, in their enthusiasm for the ranch, remind us of where we live.

And what of old growth I cannot see but know? As an adolescent, I thought God was a personal god, one who "answered my prayers." In my young mind, I made an estimate of all the people in the world, and concluded he could not. I once thought all I wanted was to have children and a home of my own. And I did, and I do. But my essential role has died out.

As Parker J. Palmer has written in *On the Brink of Everything*: "We can learn from autumn, when the falling and dying we see all around us are, in fact, seeding a season of rebirth. Autumn in the natural world reminds us that the 'little deaths' we experience in the autumn of our lives, and the 'big death' that will happen when we go over the brink, are necessary for new life to emerge." "Life 'composts' and 'seeds' us as autumn does the earth."[19]

And as Erik Erickson, developmental psychologist and psychoanalyst, postulated in his theory on the life stages of man, successful navigation of one's later years requires an acceptance of two opposing forces. Between forty and sixty-five, he suggests we travel in the world of care: for our families, for our work. At the end of that period, we are faced with a choice between generavity and stagnation. Generavity referring to the act of contributing to the well-being of family and community with whatever gifts one has to offer.

And later, in a period he refers to as "Wisdom"—age sixty-five and up—we are faced with a choice between integrity and despair. Erickson believes that in the management of the tension between those forces we come to a reconciliation of the reality of our lives, and in that way, we maintain a healthy perspective as we age.

I find his work most helpful in the idea of "ego-integrity," the ability to accept life in its fullness as it is, in its successes and failures. We navigate our way to a state of wisdom when we can embrace an "informed and detached concern for life itself in the face of death itself."[20]

And here is my new work, the new growth that must come out of the old: to negotiate the reality of regrets with the gift of living a reasonably good life now, and then turn and look to all that awaits me.

Once Emma, Griz, and I finish our circuitous routes around the lawns, I put the hand rakes away and park the harrow and the four-wheeler at the equipment shed, ready for the next chore. Content, I walk to the house.

TWENTY-ONE

In Cathedral Light

BELOW FARWELL MOUNTAIN, A BRAWNY RISE COVERED in aspen and pine, friends of ours, Jim and Barb, oversee the Bootjack Ranch. Jim irrigates and hays the meadows come summer and leases hillsides to the Sand Mountain Cattle Company for grazing their Red Angus.

In Jim and Barb's homestead cabin, tucked in at the back of the draw, Barb's sitting room houses reading time in the afternoons and Pearl Lake secreted in the view. Just beyond their home, a one-room bunkhouse serves as Barb's studio. There her easels hold watercolor canvases washed in forest, mountain, columbine, and daffodil.

Come early spring, it is here, at the Bootjack that ranchers and old friends gather for Jim's spring equinox celebration. Throughout the year, he gathers and cleans the refuse from his land. Recently, two building projects—a garage for Barb and a shop for Jim—left many woody remains. In recent years, Jim, with the help of modern-day lumberjacks, removed more than five hundred beetle killed pine trees from their land, adding to the woody remains. At the same time, they mourned over the loss of much of their Bootjack forest.

The winters are long below Farwell. Snow depths reach four and five feet on the level. Dry ground may not appear until the end of May. So, in mid-March, I'm not surprised when the phone rings. Jim and Barb anxiously await the sun's return. "Mary, it's Jim. I'm starting the call around for the bonfire. What works for you?"

After a couple of tries, Jim calls from his wall phone and says, "Looks like the twenty-fourth works. We'll see you about six. Don't forget to bring what you want to toss in the fire."

Each year for more than twenty-years we've shared in smoked

meats, deviled eggs, baked beans, bread, and Barb's homemade cherry and apple pies. Jim sets his table with daffodils beribboned in mason jars, collared in Easter grass, and dotted with hand-dyed eggs in yellow, blue, and red, each a wishful symbol: blue for clear sky, red for warmth, and yellow for longer days and shorter nights.

After dinner, one by one we file out of the homestead house, bundled in Carharts, boots, mittens, and hats. At the foot of the steel-grated steps, Jim lights the torch—a scrap of lumber wrapped in cloth and soaked in diesel fuel. Each year a different leader lights the way to the bonfire, some years honored for youth, some for age. Ceremoniously lit, Jim hands the torch to the bearer.

In a quiet procession, we reach the grand pyramid not too far from the house. Even though the load settles beneath the deep winter snows, it remains imposing above the snowpack. Once we encircle the stack, the torch bearer hands the flare to Jim. Beginning with last year's Christmas tree, he strikes the giant match until the flames won't be turned back. In recent years, Jim, a quiet man, takes delight in his undercover shenanigans. Without a word and minutes into the flame, firecrackers shout out and children exclaim, "Lookout, wow, did you see that!"

As the fire settles and slows from its eruption, we stand in its warmth, the adults communing, the children boisterous with snowballs and wrestling in snowpack where no one gets hurt. Either made snug in a pocket or in a hand, most of us carry a token of a winter burden. In the early years, long underwear or worn out winter work gloves were often tossed in. School-aged children might have sent a flurry of papers, old tests, or the effigy of a difficult teacher into the inferno.

It's not always said what goes into the fire. Men seldom surrender a symbol of their winter. On occasion, I may pursue what's on their mind and ask, "So what would you throw in?" Recently, a rancher and an old friend said, "The month of January."

However, most of the women write theirs down. With each season, the burdens shift. In memory of losing her mother one year, a friend sent a copy of her mother's sheet music into the flame. Several years ago, I carried a file, representative of the red tape of my mother's estate, onerous all winter long. Another friend writes in small script on a remnant of paper her grief over the loss of her family's Kansas farm. Carefully folded or simply carried bare, the tokens are delivered as close to the heat as possible. Then with a quick fling, they're gone.

Each year I hold my token away from the fire before I throw it in. I reflect on its presence in my life as I stand between the light of the inferno and the dark of night. As though in prayer, I know the feeling when the token is consumed; the temporal and precious space for transformation in the meditation disappears too.

As I commune with others in the heat, I stand in the light of a cathedral. I find it's not just the releasing of the token that night or the winter weight taken up in the smoke and ash of the blast, but the ritual of preparing for the fire and standing with children and old friends that fashions the renewal. As the fire begins to ease and the night grows deeper into the woods beyond the flame, we turn back to the house. Our procession quiet, as though peace settled over the Bootjack and visited each one of us.

TWENTY-TWO

LEAVE IT

OVER THE YEARS AS A MOTHER, I WAS ENTICED, NOW and then, into thinking I knew just what to do. Whether it was discipline, decisions, or problem-solving, I frequently thought I knew what path should be taken. The fall of 1997 comes easily to mind.

It's November. My son, Andy, is a senior in high school. College applications are due in two weeks. "Andy, have you finished up that last essay? Did you download the application for an in-state school?"

"Mom, I'm not goin' to an in-state school. If I don't get into Montana or Cal Poly, I'm not goin'."

"But, Andy, you have to. You know what they say about tiers of schools."

Andy never applies to an in-state school.

I lay awake at night through early December. What will he do if he doesn't get in? Will he ever go? How will he live?

I wish I had known my Boston Terrier, Emma then.

Emma's paws rest under her chin as she waits for a treat from our trainer. Valerie kneels on the floor in front of her, points her finger at Emma and says, "Leave it." Just inches from Emma's nose, the doggie treat is a great temptation for a six-month-old puppy. Emma's eyes look intently at Valerie and then my way, as if to say, "What do I do?"

The scent of the treat drifts over Emma. Overcome by temptation she pulls herself part way up to take it. Valerie quickly reprimands her, "No, Emma. This isn't for you right now. Leave it." And Emma lays back down. The second trial succeeds as Emma waits just a few seconds before Valerie's release, "Get it, Emma." Emma instantly enjoys her treat.

I always admired her discipline to obey my "Leave It" command, most often when we walked along our county road or into the hills above the ranch. One recent afternoon the sun warmed just enough to break the bite out of the breeze.

Glimpses of stubby oat and sand meadow grass catch my eye. Spring is near and Emma, Griz, and I begin. Our daily walk never abandons its ritual. The dogs sprint a hundred yards down the county road to the hay shed. Turn in, spin, and race back out to the road. Then off we go. Griz trots as though a handsome soldier. Emma races, screeches, and searches for scents.

The mound on the side of the road up ahead invited speculation all winter. Buried beneath plowed snow, its placement and shape indicated something other than an old clump of roadside grass. Emma always inspected it. I didn't worry. She couldn't get into it—until today.

Off she goes. I see her sniff, paw, and then tug. A few steps closer I see the remains of a badger, its coarse hair matted, and its raccoon eyes faint but visible. I yell, "Leave it, Emma, leave it!" The old carcass, a find to Emma, a source of concern to me. If Emma rolls in it, she'll need a bath. If Emma eats it, she may get sick.

Emma looks my way. I think I hear her say, "Yeah, but. Yeah, but." Emma looks back at the badger, takes a step closer, sniffs, and looks my way again. "Leave it, Emma." And Emma walks away. Griz looks back, sees us coming and knows we'll carry on happily down the road.

If I had known Emma's obedience command "leave it," I may have slept at night when Andy refused to apply to those schools. I may have let go of my fear and placed my trust in him, the son we had raised. For Andy did find his own path. Andy graduated from California Polytechnic University. Andy lives and works here on the ranch. Andy is a husband and father.

But while Emma modeled the strength it takes to leave things that don't need my guidance or, in my mind, are falsely controlled by my will, I confess I have yet to master the deeper nuances of the discipline.

During my mother's last December of life, I bring her flowers. Sometimes a bouquet from the grocery store or on special occasions, an arrangement from a florist. The grocery store staff tells me, "Of course, roses go quickly and cosmos, too, but artemisia, baby's breath, and carnations last the longest." Today I brought Christmas sugar cookies, too, wrapped in beribboned cellophane.

I walk down the hall of the nursing home. "Your mom will be so happy to see you!" In her wheelchair, my mother is parked in the doorway of her room. She loves travel. She loves people. Today, where would she go and who would she see if she could?

"Oh, you're here! Such pretty f lowers!"

Handing her the bouquet, "Can I turn you around, and we'll get those f lowers in the light of the window?"

Her reply is so soft I assume it's a "yes." Her quiet in her voice sounds as though her breath can no longer carry the strength of her heart.

As I walk into her room, I see that her newspapers and books have gathered on her desk and her Bible is closed. I open the cellophane sack of cookies. "Would you like one? Don't they make you feel like a kid again?" She shakes her head, "I don't think so."

I feel my chest collapse ever so slightly as though a small hopeful child wanting to fix the hurt. She used to love to eat.

Each time I visited, I kept hoping something would change her life, keep her mind bright, her eyes clear, and loneliness at bay. I kept hoping she'd pick up the news and her daily, faithful readings. I kept hoping whatever I brought her or could offer her would keep her alive.

As I held vigil over my mother's last days, it became clear to me it was not her pending death that I grieved so much as the loss of knowing and admiring her drive for life. To witness it seep out against her will laid bare my powerlessness to push back death. It was as Scott Russell Sanders describes his wife's father's last days in *The Force of Spirit*: "To say that he is dying makes it sound as though he's doing something active, like singing or dancing, but really something is being done to him. Life is leaving him." The cycle of life and death is a clear path. Pushing, tugging, and railing against its end comes to no end.

I may always need Emma's command. It's now three-and-a-half years later, and I still hear my mind chattering, wishing I could have remedied her suffering and loneliness the last six months of her life. But I couldn't. Death comes. The end of life is in possession of its own path. The only path I must make is my own each day; and then, like Emma, I will carry on down the road, through my day, greeting the fullness of both the light and dark of life.

TWENTY-THREE

A Rustling in the Oaks

FTER THE DEATH OF A WRITER FRIEND, I ATTENDED her memorial service at the edge of Steamboat Lake not far from where I live. The presiding pastor, dressed in a red plaid western shirt and black Wranglers, wore his long gray hair in a ponytail. With a brisk September wind to his back and with kind assurance, he ended his blessing with, "Her spirit is now a footprint in the snow, an echo in the mountain whenever she's near."

Sarah, a tall, elegant, and athletic blond in her fifties, lost a fierce six-month battle with cancer and told no one until the last six weeks of her life. I found comfort in the pastor's words. Still struggling with the finality of my mother's death earlier in the year, the notion of her spirit "an echo in the mountain" drew me in.

At ninety-four, my once hearty mother dies on a cold January night. The wind blows, ice forms on window panes and sidewalks. After her last labored breath, my sister and I call the funeral home. In the darkened hallway, I thought I'd walked into the wrong movie when Jerry, the tall funeral director, dressed in a long, black overcoat, arrives with his gurney furnished with a red plush blanket.

During the last week of her life, we hold close vigil over her—playing her favorite hymns, rubbing her hands and face with lotion, and welcoming friends, family, and Pastor John who softly chants Christian blessings at her bedside. When death comes, my sister and I spend a few moments with her after the nurses' aides gently straighten her up and support her head with a towel so we can remember her—

not as a crumpled body on its side—but as our mother, dignified in death.

After formalities with Jerry, my sister and I gather our mother's Bible and a vase of still-fresh flowers, curl up in our coats, walk through the back door of Fair Acres Manor and down an icy sidewalk slope to my car. Jerry escorts my mother through the front door on the mortuary's gurney, covered in red velvet. I imagine in the elegant contours the last physical evidence of her existence, of her life in this world.

I often watch for signs of life when I wander on a nearby hill. I've come to know a small ecosystem exists hidden from view. The oak- and chokecherry-covered ground rests between the open meadows below and the aspen groves neighboring the evergreen forest above on the ridge. The wildlife native to my home come and go, graze, sleep, retreat in the shadows of the brush, the shade of the aspen when safe, curled in the sparse grass on the soil-poor ground. I take pleasure in searching for evidence of that small world.

When winter arrives and the earth is layered in down, I eagerly follow the spoor on the snowshoe trail. Following in the footsteps of ancient hunters and gatherers who tracked for food, I know it's important to know the rhythms and patterns of the landscape in which I wander. The intimate knowledge of knowing when and where the elk winter and breed; where the birds flutter, light, and sing; where the ermine burrow lower on the hill; and where the porcupine often hides in the brush help me know where to cast my search.

The days of tracking are never the same. I know when elk hoof prints disappear into heavy brush, crisscrossing the slope, grazing through one draw to the next, they have settled for the winter on the face of the hill. I often step across their lays, beds used only once or twice. Deep and curved, with a close look, hair from the elk's hide resides inside. As the elk depart, they frequently leave more evidence in pellet-shaped droppings, shiny if fresh.

While nuthatches winter in Colorado and often forage with chickadees, I don't see them every year. But when I do, their tracks form the most delicate of imprints. Their slender toes, three to the front and one to the back, only brush the surface but tell the story of a landing, exploration, and then flight. I assume they are on the hill for pleasure, perhaps looking for a spare seed to tuck away in the seam of cottonwood when they return to their nest.

The ermine, an American short-tailed weasel in its dense, silky white winter coat, is known as a predator to rodents, rabbits, and native bird populations. I am taken by the diminutive ermine paw prints that bound from beneath the oak down the path to the next safe haven, an oak brush well, maybe the cover of a sparse, winter sage. The delicate prints camouflage the true nature of the ermine who killed the rabbit or rodent and then pirated their home.

In the tracking of the wildlife on the hill, there's an intimacy I treasure. While I seldom see the elk on the rise or over the ridge deep in the aspen, the nuthatch perched in the oak, the ermine tucked and curled in its burrow, or the porcupine gnawing his dinner, I see testimonials to their existence. To know I am accompanied by creatures that share the well-worn path, I feel connected to the ground we share, bound to the same oak and chokecherry-covered hill.

On a cold and crisp January morning, while working on my mother's eulogy, I stand at my kitchen window, waiting for tea water to boil. Having been told of a Native American custom to notice the first wildlife to pass by after a loved one's death, I watch carefully through the window.

In stillness, a bald eagle sails at treetop above the gray, barren cottonwoods. It's not unusual to see them sailing above the river. They live near, nesting up high just below the crown of the tree. As I watch the slow and free wingbeats of the eagle that morning, I imagine my mother free, sailing north on a light breeze. I entertain the thought that her spirit might also see me there at the kitchen window. At that moment, I name the eagle steward of my mother's spirit, a healing talisman.

I later learn that the belief birds embody the spirits of the dead is an ancient belief, crossing many cultures. The Buddhists made rice offerings to ancestral "house spirits" that were then eaten by birds; and in India, a similar ritual is performed for crows.[21]

Research suggests man inherently seeks to understand the birds as symbolic of both life and death: some represent fertility; some portend imminent death; and others suggest the human spirit lives on in the avian world. These beliefs, according to Moreman, "cross cultures through human history." In Moreman's study of the relationship between birds and spirits of the dead, he posits that the underlying human drive to do so is to deny the finality of death, to soothe the angst of our own personal mortality.[22]

While the absence of her physical presence continues to stir me— as though I've lost contact with my origin—whenever I see the bald eagle sailing the river or crossing overhead, the reminder helps fill the space left empty by her death. In the moment I'm reminded she will never leave me: her love of books, her love of people, her laughter, her loyal presence, and sharp mind are still a part of me.

The bald eagle, not unlike the rustling of the oaks, tells of the existence of a life I cannot see. And whether it's the wildlife nearby or my mother's spirit, I rest on the testament and willingly fall into the embrace of those who are now out of view but with whom I've traveled through this earthly life.

A SEASON TURNS

TWENTY-FOUR

THE RIVER WANES

ROMEO'S BACK SWAYS. THAT IS TO SAY IT'S SLACK AND loose. His withers protrude and his coat in the winter is shaggy. When my daughter, Cassidy, was sixteen, she bought Romeo, a black gelding reminiscent of Black Beauty.

When the wind picks up and stirs the horses in the pastures south of the house, the movement catches my eye through the kitchen window. No one would ever know the gelding who charges, gallops, twirls, and kicks up his heels is the oldest horse on the ranch. Romeo is now twenty-six.

Come Christmas, when Cassidy and her husband visit and the day quiets from the rustling of shiny paper, she goes to the refrigerator for carrots and an apple. She bundles up in her Carharts and winter boots, fluffy hat, and warm gloves. When Romeo hears her call, he comes to the gate. He still remembers her voice and her Christmas day gift.

His retirement to a lush meadow in the summer is well earned. He was loyal and good and dependable. A friend. A willing partner. An all-around good guy. The winter now, however, is hard on him, particularly the cold. He needs extra nourishment in a special ration of grain to keep him healthy.

As I lingered in bed recently, enjoying the slow morning rise, I imagined living my life again, to inhabit the scenes in real time. The longing seemed to be shaped at first by nostalgia, but in the end, I knew it rested in the awareness my life, now past the mid-point, tapers to the end without my permission. I shut my eyes and allowed the desire to go back, to reclaim, if only for a brief time that morning.

There was nothing more that I wanted in my young life than to have children. Before Andy and Cassidy left home, their lives marked my time, defined the weeks, seasons, and years. When I recently ran across a photo taken of them before the county fair in 1996, it captured a sweet memory I carried with me for several days.

It wasn't unusual for them to "exercise" their 4-H steers behind an old, beat-up, faded yellow Willys jeep. In the photo, Andy stands on the back bumper with a hand on the halter, his steer following, cooperating for his daily walk. Both were at the mercy of Cassidy at the steering wheel, who at the time was twelve years old.

Ranch. Animals. Work. Self-sufficiency. Cooperation. Each was still a child. Each had the other. Dependent yet for some time, they were, in my reminiscence, on the verge of knowing they would be independent one day. And in the end, that's all I wanted.

As I look back, I wonder: did I do good things? make the most of my days and my life? The timeline feels hollow as though I failed to fill it in. I feel the years slip through like the run-off in the spring, vanishing downstream and beyond.

I see the early turning of the cottonwood, aspen, serviceberry, chokecherry and dogwood. The sun tips and they follow. I watch the raspberries. If not picked, they darken, retreat from their cream conical roost and then they have no choice but to drop from their hold. The bed of the raspberry patch is always littered with forgotten berries. I feel guilty. I hadn't gathered them in time.

When I am disturbed about something in my life, I read. I search for wise perspectives to act as a backdrop for the unsettling scene. Jean Amery, a European journalist, writes of aging in a series of essays: "There is the matter of time. When we are young, we stand in the middle of both space and time, but as we grow older our sense of space disappears and time alone crowds in on us, becomes in fact a characteristic of daily existence; we think about time all the time."[23] What potential have we? Have our accomplishments already been counted?

In recent years, I take heart, in part, believing Pete and I continue in our work of maintaining the ranch, which serves a nexus of sorts for our children and extended family who have spent time here. A niece and nephew who experienced unsettling change as children wear their memories of the ranch like a talisman, steadying their identity as a member of the clan, the tribe, claiming an enduring home ground.

The heart of our work created a niche for our family story. We carved, cleared, built, and filled in. When we arrived in 1986, there were no evergreens, no aspen grove, no lawns, just homesteader's lilac, poppy, and a few rhubarb. Our house was yet to be built and the bunkhouse and homestead house yet to be salvaged. The trail from the house to the barn was yet to be tamped down, embedded midst the cottonwoods and across the small creek. The barn was just four stalls and filled with previous owners' leftovers—tack, harness, saddles, old posts, newspapers, oil cans, tires, fifty-gallon drums.

Today, the blue spruce we planted outside the kitchen window in the spring of 1987 is forty feet tall, its boughs extending fifteen feet in circumference. With the help of a builder who specializes in historic restorations, the barn has additional wings, one to each side—one an equipment stall, the other for foaling stalls. The open pastures once used for grazing sheep have been partitioned into paddocks for different groups of horses, a few buffalo, and others for the domestic elk we once raised.

As young settlers of sorts, we aspired, we hoped, we dug into this valley as though ermine in a burrow moving moist soil this way and that, clearing a passage for shelter, carved and curved for safety and warmth, space enough for young, and a full life. And now with our indwelling secure, our young sufficient, do we move on? And if we do, what kind of burrow would we carve?

> The anxiety about death both contributes to one's sense of utter helplessness and buttresses one's need to take responsibility for the time she has.[24]
>
> —Ruth Garfield

As I reflect on the challenge of accepting fewer years ahead of me than behind me, I think of Griz. He isn't supposed to be alive. Over a year ago, he was diagnosed with a nasal tumor, an acute growth of cancerous cells making it difficult to breathe. When I came downstairs for morning coffee, I would find spots and smears of blood on the floor seeping from his nose where he had sleep during the night. He could no longer hike on the hill. He could no longer live the life he knew.

But technology at Colorado State University Veterinary Hospital would give him more life. With palliative radiation, a radiation that shrinks the tumor but doesn't guarantee its full remission, he was given back his life. Dr. Wormhudt told us the treatment would give him six to eight months more to live. Griz had only a 17 percent chance of surviving beyond that. When she delivered the news, I focused on the 17 percent survival rate and thought out loud, "Why not Griz?" She smiled, consoling as though to say, "Well, maybe, but..." And I nodded, "Yes, I know."

> *Much of the appeal of Montaigne lies in the way in which, as you turn the pages, you can hear the incessant click-click of life's cyclometer. Instead of taking time's passing clicks merely as a countdown to disaster, Montaigne is fascinated by the cargoes that they carry.*[25]
>
> —Chris Arthur

Now, nearly eighteen months later, Griz is still alive. He's part of a long-term study on palliative radiation at the University of Saskatchewan. We know each day he's on borrowed time. But Grizzy doesn't know he lives on borrowed time. He just lives each day hoping to fill each moment. He greets me at the bottom of the stairs and waits for his morning tummy rub. He waits for me to open the door for his early morning venture outside. And then Griz sits on the deck at daybreak and continues to watch over his place. He continues to say, "Let's go. Time's a'wastin!" He seems to have heard Montaigne. It's not the clicks of the clock, it's the "cargoes," the contents of the moments of each day that matter as we age.

Mid-October, Pete stands on an extended ladder and paints white trim on the horse stalls. A longtime friend and rancher, Jay Fetcher, drives into the barnyard in his small, red Toyota pick-up with Nellie, his golden retriever. "So, are you painting because you have to or because you want to?" Both men are negotiating the passing of their ranching operations to the next generation.

"You know, I'm paintin' because I have to. I'm paintin' because I need to. And I'm paintin' because I want to."

And they both smile.

As we age, we wonder if we can do the work, and we imagine leaving and moving to town. Perhaps a small home in the middle of things where we could walk to the park, library, and pool. But we conclude that until the work is impossible to manage, we are sustained by the work, the need to be a part of things each day. We look forward to the relief a ranch manager would bring. And that step will be essential in the coming months. But chores offer structure and purpose and, in this way, meaning. This is what we do. And we carry on as though the demands, albeit with great weight at times, are those cargoes Montaigne acknowledged and Grizzy so eagerly carried.

I return to my daily journal.

The river wanes overnight, the temperatures settle around the mid-forties, and the tips of cottonwoods and willows, sensitive to the daily light, soften to yellow. The season has tipped, passed its mid-point and all the elements that make it shift, the essence of summer drifting, loosening, transforming into the essence of another, the same elements at work, only a different shade of each: light, temperature, a tilting earth.

TWENTY-FIVE

RESTORATION

FALL IN LOVE WITH A BIRDHOUSE AT THE HARDWARE STORE. I examine the stone replica of an English house, complete with chimney, black roof, red-trimmed windows, red front door and wish perhaps I might live there. I purchase the house and take it home. With Pete's help, I reclaim an old birdhouse post and drive it into the soft, shaded ground in the aspens and cottonwoods on the east side of the house. Pete screws the stone replica onto the post, and I wait for the first residents.

Ten years later, I see the peeling paint and the roof and platform askew. Should I throw it away? I conclude that there might not be another nest to use. I unscrew the birdhouse from its metal post and take it to the shop. I sand. I paint. I realign the roof. This morning, outside my kitchen window, the reclaimed house hosts sparrows undercover, slipping in and out.

Reclaim

Not until 1978 did I arrange a small four-by-eight-foot garden in full sun by the back door of our first home. I never practiced gardening as a child even though I watched my mother tend her irises along my childhood home just footsteps from the backdoor; and I watched my father trim the roses he'd planted around an evergreen in our front yard. Each Christmas he made a wreath of greens from that tree.

My first gardening year I planted carrots, potatoes, onions, strawberries, and green beans. For the next thirty-nine years, I tended my gardens: tilled their beds, planted short-season seeds, and then harvested potatoes, tomatoes, rhubarb, and greens.

But the physical labor wore on my hands, particularly my left hand. The sharp pain of bone on bone in my thumb and lightning bolts of nerve pain up and down my index finger made weeding and pruning perennials a difficult task. So I hired Erin, a woman who maintains gardens for homeowners, to trim, weed, and clear dead growth. While I love her assistance, I always feel apologetic that I can't help.

As she lifts the remains of a long winter season from the gardens, I continue with a lighter hand. I lay diminutive seeds in furrowed rows of my vegetable garden. I plant pots for the ranch—geraniums and vines in whiskey barrels, an old hot water tank, and numerous pots at the arena, barn, and bunkhouse. In the arranging and settling the roots into their containers, I love listening to the ways the color, height, and texture ask to be together.

The discomfort, however, continued whether I worked in the garden or in the house. Intolerable—an accidental knock of my hand against a hard surface or someone's overly enthusiastic grasp of my hand. I conceded and elected a complicated hand surgery.

A skilled surgeon fuses my left basal thumb joint, an arthrodesis. He replaces the eroded trapezium bone with a small, triangular bone carved from my wrist. Setting it precisely in place, he plates and screws the substitute. The bone eventually befriended other metacarpal bones. While my thumb moves with relative ease now, my open palm will never lay flat.

And next, the ambitious task of placing an implant in the metacarpophalangeal joint (MCP) of my index finger, still feels audacious. The phalanges joining my index finger trimmed and a titanium post and silicone ball tucked in, one to each end, and glued in place. The procedure, an arthroplasty, translates literally to "re-forming of the joint."

My MCP joint may be reformed, but my index finger doesn't go around and around anymore. I struggle with the hinge, unlike the miraculous rotation of a ball and socket. I feel the side pressure when I pick up a reusable grocery bag filled with apples, onions, and greens; twist off caps and lids; or pick up my granddaughter. So, I remind myself—it's almost automatic now—of my surgeon's request: "It's called bypass. We like you to bypass the joint whenever possible." And he demonstrates the pinching of, not the thumb and index finger, but the thumb and second finger.

I shouldn't complain. It's not difficult. No more bone on bone; no more nerve lightning bolts up and down my finger. While grateful for the repair, a small anger rises not quite a year after surgery, a rebellion against the limitations physical repairs impose. They are never perfect.

Like my surgeon, I feel audacious. I walk out into a thick August afternoon and grab my shovel. I step back in to the perennial gardens to prune and weed small trimmings and plants. I dig up and rip out old friends: snow in summer and moss pinks. So tangled with one another, their individuality collapsed. I save a clump of moss pinks and transplant them to the foreground of another garden.

Snow in summer, a greedy perennial, takes up more than its share of space everywhere it takes root. I throw it into the burn pile, a pyramid of remains from ranch work: lumber, trimmings, perhaps an animal carcass—calf, woodchuck, or deer—flesh the dogs shouldn't find. I uproot other interlopers too: Canadian thistle, dandelions, arrogant meadow grass, and leggy foreign weeds and toss them into the burn pile too.

I look back on the last six years and think: *I not only relinquished the labor, I lost something else.* Caretaking the ranch landscape provided a purpose on the ranch in the summertime after my children left home. In handing over the heavier caretaking, I also distance myself emotionally from my gardens. I unconsciously protect myself from a loss I could not control. I'd rationalize: *You can still enjoy the landscape even though you can't do it all.*

I continue cutting back the shasta daisies and Russian sage. Then, standing back to view the renewal—the clear spaces, the trimmed plants, and fresh, fragrant cedar mulch—I remember the intimacy in creating and tending. The work, one between the dependent and the aegis, the protector, like a mother to her young, filled the void. I knew each plant, where it lived, when it bloomed, how timid, how resilient. Tears, liminal at first, rise. I press my small shovel to unearth the next clump of errant grass. I hadn't known what I'd lost until I returned.

With deliberation, I take my risk. Easy on the pull and twist of the plant or weed. Easy on the lift of the wood handle as I dig, and that evening, heat and Aleve. My hand back at work. My heart tending again.

Renew

I head to the shop for a gallon of redwood stain for the front porch. We'd offered to host a family reunion at the ranch for my mother's side of the family. Four generations of family members, eighty guests from a dozen states, Central America, and Denmark confirmed their arrival in late July.

The ranch hadn't been renovated for a decade. The demands of each summer season—keeping equipment running, daily irrigating chores, fencing, and haying—never allowed much time or energy to clean up and restore.

So, in the summer of 2010 our list was long: paint and stain for our home, cabin, and sheds; new wires and posts for fences; fresh mulch for tree rings and new perennials—salvia and lupine—and finally, road base for our potholed driveway. When the weather settled in May after a moody spring in northwestern Colorado, we began.

I dip my brush into the gallon can and let the bristles soak in as much stain as they might carry. I fail to remember how many years it's been since this threshold has been a focus of attention; invisible to our comings and goings, we open the door and look beyond the stoop to the guest, the UPS man, or our next chore waiting for us down the trail.

So, I kneel down to cover the aged wood with stain. Its stringent, sweet smell of colorants and solvent drift and then repel. I begin with the first two steps. I soon recall a photo of Cassidy standing just below on the concrete pad on the first day of kindergarten. She wore a blue calico dress and around her neck a large sign with her name spelled in large letters. Cassidy looked up at the camera holding the sign with both hands, one eye squinting as if to turn something back. Her discomfort seemed to ask, "Will I be OK?"

Extremely shy as a child, I knew the pain of being in the world. So, I worried about her too. Even though she attended two-day a week pre-school with caring teachers, I stirred with questions later that morning after I sent her through the kindergarten door. Should I have held her back? Had I not paid enough attention to her discomfort? At her first conference, her teacher says, "Oh, she's fine. She's capable of the work and she seems happy."

I work my way from the steps to the landing, slowly pressing each stroke deliberately down each plank. As I carefully draw the brush over the lip of the landing and back again, I think of Andy. A memorable exchange from his adolescence occurred here, right at the edge of the porch.

Pete and I repeated the dangers of cigarettes and alcohol as though a mantra to our children. However, at sixteen, I'd found chewing tobacco in Andy's laundry. I was dismayed. Pete and I made a deep commitment to sound behavior management in parenting our children.

During the years of Andy developing will at two and three, I offered choices. "It's time to get dressed. You can wear this outfit or this one. You choose." When he went out on the weekends in high school, he had a curfew. It was his responsibility to return home in time to turn off an alarm set for his curfew outside our bedroom door. He never missed a curfew.

But children often provide a humbling, disruptive ground, one in which to stumble. Our enlightened parenting had resulted in a soggy bag of Red Man in my laundry room. At that moment, I'm the one filled with the spin of a tantrum. Rarely had I ever let lose my words.

Andy, off work one afternoon from his job at the local feed store, walks to his red Dodge pick-up. I follow him out the door. Standing on the edge of the porch, "You know you're a dumb shit for using chewing tobacco." His mother had gone over the edge. Only later in his life did I hear, "I was just so shocked to hear you lose it. And in the moment, I knew you must be right."

In the art of restoration, whether it's a front porch, a piece of furniture, or a piece of jewelry, when the restorer ushers the article back to its original condition, it's as though it's brought back into existence. Memories, tucked away, returned to the steps and the lip of the landing that day.

After the front porch, I trimmed trees, planted pots, and returned our twenty-five-year-old trampoline back to its original color with thick, shiny blue paint. Pete and our hired hand stained the house, painted outbuildings, oversaw the driveway leveled with road base, and nailed top rails back where they belonged. With the ranch renewed, we awaited our guests.

Reunite

I raise a Danish flag above the old sawmill cabin we use for social events at the ranch. Inside, with the help of my sister, I check in, "All set? Did we get everyone's orders for reunion hats and shirts organized?" Later in the day, family would arrive for our first dinner together. The Mortensens know how to gather. We'd come together every two years for over twenty years. The commitment to family began with my maternal grandparents.

My grandfather emigrated from a dark life in Denmark. At seventeen he boarded the *Empress of Ireland* with passage in third class. Two older brothers awaited his arrival in Iowa. My grandmother's family, the Ides and the Cottons, settled in America in the 1700s. Her mother died young, but she adored her father. A progressive, civic-minded Iowa business man, he, at the turn of the century, saved enough money for all of his three daughters' college educations. However, a medical condition in adolescence required my grandmother's admittance to a sanitarium at the expense of her college fund. Faithfully, her father stood by her, visited her regularly while she recovered.

The cars roll in along the newly leveled driveway. Nieces and nephews, aunts and uncles, first wives, second wives, and third generation newborns slip out and, in an instant, I see second cousins headed for the blue trampoline. "Did you get your name tag and shirt? Head over to the cabin and sign in. Make sure you sign up for the blind man's tractor race too!"

Of the eighty guests, a dozen arrived from Denmark. Through an admiration of the *émigré* story perhaps, links to my grandfather's family remained tight, secure, of utmost importance. His cousin, Aunt Laura, who remained in Denmark, maintained connection in the early years through letters to known relations in America.

The Mortensens gathered before in Alborg, Denmark, in 1989, my grandfather's home ground. Upon our arrival there, outside the window of the bus, I see a woman who looks like my mother waiting to cross the street. My second Danish cousin and I sit together at a farmhouse dinner. From across the room, "Hey, you two look alike!" What is it about family, familiarity, and the maintenance of such?

In retirement, my grandparents regularly visited Michigan, New York, Arizona, and Colorado to "catch up" with Uncle Joe, Uncle Jim, my parents, and any other relative nearby. In preparation for their arrival, the host would stock up on Post Toasties for my grandfather and pull out the Scrabble board for my grandmother. They came annually to the ranch until my grandfather's death in 1983.

As host, I stocked up, too, with the help of caterers, of course, and the delivery service of now grown nephews. "They said it would be ready for pick-up at five. Could you make a trip into town?"

"I'm on my way."

"I hope you all like Qdoba! Let's eat!"

I sit with my Uncle Jim and his second wife, Brenda, at a ten-top table in the party tent. He shows signs of fatigue and early dementia.

A paratrooper in World War II and successful Manhattan business man, I feel a gentleness in him I recognize as my grandmother's, as though she's still here.

Around the campfire, refrains of our family history echo: stories of the immigrant, so proud of his employment with the United States Railway Service, he wore a white dress shirt and slacks beneath his working overalls; and of my grandmother, the formidable Scrabble competitor who couldn't contain her pleasure with each 'gotcha' move.

Around the campfire, too, though, other stories fail to surface, the ones family members survived, but speak little of.

Beloved father of Mabel Ide Mortensen
and
The first-born son of Mabel Ide and Axel Mortensen
Pass away on the same day
d. July 3, 1936

Linda A. Mortensen
d. August 20, 1974
Succombs to brain cancer and leaves
Joseph Ide Mortensen and three children

Mary Janet Mortensen Burman
Wife to Robert, mother to James, Edward, and John
Cared for each as they succumbed to spinocerebellar ataxia

Robert D. Burman	d. June 2, 2003
James Robert Burman	d. April 11, 1995
Edward Ide Burman	d. May 21, 1998
John M. Burman	d. February 21, 2019

The late summer evening lingers and draws down Saturday night. I and others light paper lanterns for those we love and lost. As they set sail, I hear Kristen, a great-granddaughter, sing "Ave Maria" and feel as though I'm traveling with the light. I see my mother sitting in a comfortable chair on the deck, wrapped snug in a blanket as though a contented child watching the lanterns' light drift to the south beyond Elk Mountain. The reunion would be my mother's last visit to the ranch.

On Sunday morning, my Uncle Joe, my mother's youngest brother and a retired Baptist minister, speaks, as he always does for our gatherings, with gentle words and voice. He reminds us, although we've suffered losses, faced confusions, and disturbances to personal peace, we have received our "goodly inheritance" from this coalescence we call family. "We are blessed," he says, "to know from where we came, to know the strength of those who persevered and survived. And in their daily living, Grandma and Grandpa gave us a model for a purposeful and compassionate life."

I look across the table to see Andy and Cassidy listening to their great uncle Joe. I imagine those sparrows nesting, the English birdhouse reclaimed and restored.

TWENTY-SIX

AWAKENING

MISSED MY MOTHER THIS PAST EASTER. SHE ALWAYS MADE hot-cross buns on Maundy Thursday for breakfast on Good Friday morning. In the Christian calendar, Good Friday marks both the end of Lent and Christ's crucifixion. The spiced sweet bun with a decorative cross represents the crucifixion and the spices for embalming Christ upon his death. I either never knew or didn't remember the Christian symbolism of my mother's hot-cross buns. Made by her hand, as she did all our bread, I loved the sweet Zante currants.

I awoke on Good Friday and considered my recipes, one using the traditional Zante currants and the other using cranberries. As I did, I ticked off the rituals of my childhood home. Many followed the Christian calendar. The lighting of Advent candles on Sunday, the shared opening of the little numbered windows of the Advent calendar, Christmas Eve Service and tomato soup for dinner, a Lenten sacrifice that I often failed to fulfill, the laying of Palms, and sunrise services on Easter Sunday.

Others were secular. Halloween costumes, Valentine mail boxes decorated with white doilies and tissue paper, and May Day baskets made with construction paper and fresh lilacs from my mother's bush at the corner of my childhood home. And perhaps, one of my favorites, mid-summer visits to the basement of Manuel's department store. There, my mother, sister, and I pulled up chairs to slanted wooden tables and looked through big books—Butterick, Simplicity, and McCalls—for patterns for school clothes. Then we'd lay a hand over bolts of fabric in corduroy, wool, and cotton, and pick our favorite colors. In a matter of a few weeks, my mother cut, seamed, and pressed skirts and shirts in time for the first days of school.

My mother's traditions—rhythmic, intimate, a heartbeat in my young life.

After my mother's memorial service in late January, I kept her cherry wood urn on the bookshelf in my office for four months until she was interred in a veteran's cemetery in western Colorado on Memorial Day weekend. She had served in the Pentagon during World War II and was eligible for a veteran's burial. My mother helped decode Japanese communications in the Pacific, and her time in Washington would remain the highlight of her life.

She now rests in a beautiful cemetery in her beloved Grand Valley. I often think about her ashes in that beautiful cherry wood box. I have yet to decipher her resting there—no face or fingers, walking shoes or Sunday suit. I often glance at a photo of her in a navy and white dress and then I see her in the cherry wood urn, all ashes, no manifestation. And when I write this, I think of Edvard Munch's scream. From body to bone, to chip and gray and black ash.

Last night I lit a fire for the evening, and as I watched it lick and pop, I wondered: *how is it that a body burns, incinerates in cremation?* I looked it up for the first time since my mother's death. I stared at the webpage. The photo of a cremator shows a furnace lit with a fire in which it burns at 1400 to 1800 degrees, with windows and openings exposing the inferno. On average it takes two hours for a body to dry, wither, burn, vaporize, and calcify. What's left is not always in small pieces and the attendant must break it up with a hoe-like rod.

How often I've thought of those who place the remains in a cardboard box on the cement block, light the fire, walk out, wait, and return. Is the sight of the transformation stirring? What do they think about in the middle of the night? Body to ash, body to ash. I still reach for her embodiment in the photo. I am the attendant, still processing the transformation.

The world shifted after my mother's death. While the course of my grief makes its own path, the face of mortality presses on me, at times with a dull, heavy weight and at others, with a new pair of eyes. When it weighs in the middle of the night, I wonder if to push against hopelessness, I must entertain the possibility that spirit survives, is recognizable in some unimaginable form.

In lighter times, when the face of mortality awakens me to this gift of life, I feel like the young color-blind boy who was given a very special pair of glasses recently—EnChroma glasses. They allowed him to see the world in full color, as though dimensions were added to the scene. Each present moment slows as I walk through my day. I see a deeper texture and green in the aspen and evergreen. I feel a breeze more intimate, whether a high wind or soft zephyr. I receive a kindness extended in the physical space of the encounter with greater warmth. The awakening born only through the loss of my mother and the quickening in my mind of my own mortality.

When archaeologists excavated the ancient city of Herculaneum in southwestern Italy, which had been buried under volcanic ash and lava since 79 CE, they found two small loaves, each with a cross, among the ruins. When I considered my recipes for hot-cross buns on Good Friday, I realize I was unearthing, reclaiming my mother through her loyal rituals. And in the reclaiming, she was brought back to life, transformed from white, gray, and black ash to immortal spirit living on in my mortal world.

TWENTY-SEVEN

SETTLING IN

WHEN THE SNOW FINALLY COVERS THE MUD AND the muck of the ranch come November, I throw everything in the washing machine: rugs, quilts, polar-fleece throws, dog bed covers, and Kitty's bed cover. Not that I don't wash them any other time of year, but in the fall, I shake out the mud season from the house. And when it's through, I welcome the fresh, crisp air.

After I replaced Kitty's clean bed cover over the foam insert that year, she didn't crawl back in. She slept on the stairs or in her favorite living room chair or tucked away under the banister in my husband's office. Each time I walked in the laundry room, where her bed sat next to her food, it was empty. I even put her in it one morning to see if she would reconnect. But no luck.

A few days later, I walked in the laundry room after my morning coffee and found Kitty asleep in the laundry room sink. She'd never slept there. I'd watched her from time to time balancing between the two sinks to drink out of the faucet, a few drips at a time, but I'd never seen her use the sink as a bed.

Kitty did fit perfectly in the stainless steel basin. Safe, too—up away from the dogs and any other traffic through the room, and when I approached to take a picture, she barely took notice. Somehow, Kitty was at home. Although, I'd washed her bed cover before, I couldn't sort out the loss she was objecting to. Was it the dirt, the matted hair, the fleece contoured to her body, or the very smells that made her bed deeply familiar to her?

In the mystery, I thought of my mother. At eighty-seven, early stages of dementia ate away at her mind and with it, her ability to make decisions for her own daily living. The landscape of her life changed not once but three times, without her consent, when her care required moving to a different facility.

In the transitions, some more difficult than others, she adjusted to her new home and bed. One spring after she fell and broke her hip at ninety-one, we watched her retreat after surgery. Surely to heal but perhaps also to befriend another step of dependence upon others. Would she come back to us? Would the light in her eyes return? Would she find comfort in another new bed?

The year my sister and I moved her into an assisted-living facility, I read *Loving What Is* by Byron Katie. While I usually record lengthy book notes, I carried just one thought with me from Katie's book: "Love what is." Her concept, grounded in cognitive behavioral therapy, presses one to challenge the thoughts and conclusions about life when it wounds and intrudes. Too often, black and white thinking, wishful thinking, fortune telling, and "awful-izing" paint one's world. With rational, ordered thinking, one's emotional life eases, resists the dramatic storytelling of the rent, the fracture, the intrusion.

Like Kitty and my mother, now that I'm in my mid-sixties, I'm protesting the changes in my life. My identity has not been as unsure since I was thirteen. I often ask, "Who is that woman in the mirror?" Arthritis, wrinkled skin, brain lags, and diminished strength create a sense of disorientation, displacement. I feel fussy and depressed. The body I depended upon for my identity and movement in the world needs restoration. I'm Kitty in the stainless steel sink. I don't want to "Love what is." I want my youth back.

I hoped Kitty's protest would end. And it did. She slipped into her bed, settled into its clean scent with the curve of her back, her head tucked in against the fleece foam border. And a few months later while visiting my mother in her new home, I asked, "How do you like it here?" Curling under a fleece throw, she said, "I like it here. I feel safe." Gratefully, she had settled in. I want to follow in their footsteps.

As a young adult I was optimistic about my future. In my linear sight, I thought of it as an expansive place, guaranteed for all time. But the optimism that made me strong in the face of early adulthood is a glimmer now. How shall I renew my enthusiasm in the new shadow of aging and mortality?

To know the disillusionments of life, and to come enchanted still.[26]

—Muriel Strode

While searching for bearings, I discovered Muriel Strode and these faithful words. At fifty-four, Muriel and her husband, Sam Lieberman, homesteaded 640 acres near Tucson, Arizona. A new beginning. They intended to replace the original wood-framed house with a stone house. For three years they walked into the desert and gathered rocks. Unfortunately, her husband succumbed to tuberculosis and the project came to an end. But Muriel remained on the homestead until her death, I assume with eyes still searching for enchantment.

I considered seeing through Muriel's eyes. To reset my perspective, and when I did, this is what came to mind: My grandson Lucca, just nine months old, crawls, no, races across the hardwood floor. Grabs my pant legs, pulls himself as far as he can. I swoop him up and hold him close. Lucca holds my face in his hands and "mouths" my cheek. I interpret his gesture, a kiss. Collins, my granddaughter, asks to be picked up and put on the trampoline. I climb onto the mat and lay down. She looks at me and wonders if I'm teasing her. Collins laughs and lays her head on me.

Enchantment.

The sun tilts from summer to fall, as it does every year, overnight. The aspens outside my office window shimmer in a late morning breeze. I wear a flannel shirt for the first time. Zip up my wind breaker before I clip into my bike. Mention to Pete the sunlit apple reds and Tuscan sun yellows near the Red Dirt Trail. Fix cilantro-lime chicken soup for dinner. And remind myself to imagine settling into the days ahead, enchanted still.

TWENTY-EIGHT

DEAN'S GARDEN

T HE LOOK RANCH SITS AT THE SOUTH END OF THE ELK
River Valley. In winter, the coldest air settles at the ranch
headquarters right off the main road. Dean Look's mother
and father settled there during the Depression, establishing one of
the many dairies that sprouted up in the thirties and forties.

Now in his mid-seventies, Dean still gardens, raises a herd of
Black Angus cattle, and puts up enough hay to get them through the
winter. With the help of his boys, who still live nearby, Dean tore
down the old family cabin after his wife Joan died and saved the
timbers, the wringer washer, and some windows and doors. They
burned what was left: torn thirties wallpaper, a crushed couch, and
wavy floors.

Joan left him ten years ago. The cutest gal in the valley when they
were young, Dean's friends liked to dance with her at the Elk River
Tavern after they were married. But she didn't leave because she was
mad or in love with someone else. She slipped away from lung cancer.

Now Dean goes to the Tavern and sits on a stool with one of his
sons or his old friend Jr. and catches up with the news. When there's a
special band, Dean still thinks men should dance with every gal on the
floor, out of respect to each one. And if you need to know any of the
history of the Elk River Valley, Dean has it catalogued in his memory.

Even though his ranch is five miles away, it's in my neighborhood,
and when the earth warms, I keep a pulse on his garden when I drive
by on my way to town. For over thirty years, I've watched in May
when Dean rolls out a front-end loader and plows down the raggedy
remains of the wintered-over garden. He clears a lovely new plot,
smoothing over fine topsoil, readying the soil canvas for his furrows.

In a day or two, he plants plenty of peas, lettuce, potatoes, and onions, and clears the weeds from his rhubarb patch. An elevated sprinkler reaches every corner of the fifteen-by-thirty-foot garden. Dean's garden in the spring looks as though, in the ordering and planting of this garden, he's committed to a New Year's resolution.

But a couple of years ago, Dean didn't plant in May. I worried he wasn't feeling well. Then in the middle of July, he plowed up a small section of the garden. I thought, *There's no way he'd plant now. It's July.*

We have a sixty- to ninety-day growing season, friendly to only the hardiest of crops, like potatoes, lettuce, broccoli, and onions. But the next day, Dean planted three rows of green peas, staked out bamboo supports, and strung green gardeners' twine onto the supports the length of each row, all ready for the upward rise of the green pea climbers.

I mused, *what was Dean thinking? What sent him to the garden in mid-July when he knows the odds are against him? What drove him to dig up the dirt, no matter what the calendar said?*

One evening I spoke with Dean about his garden. "How is it you're a gardener? Was your mother a gardener?"

"Yes, Mom grew and canned spinach, peas, beets, and carrots. My grandmother too. In the twenties and thirties, she grew enough to hand out to neighbors who didn't have enough to feed their kids. There were some real hardships then."

"So why do you plant each spring? It's so cold at your place."

With a quiet laugh, "I suppose I want to see things come up. I used to plant lots of lettuce for Joan. She liked salads. I like to plant mostly vegetables. Peas are my favorite. But I don't always get to those weeds. It's harder some days now."

I began to think about my own gardening life. In the seventies, I dug up a small backyard plot when Pete and I were first married. I filled simple rows with carrots and lettuce seeds and Russet seed potatoes. Then, in 1979, when we moved to the ranch, he and I were swept up in a homesteading movement. With great optimism, I planted a thirty-by-forty-foot garden. I grew not all our food, but most of our food. I was certain of this.

I quickly searched for gardening tutors and found them in my local extension agent, the late Sam Haslem and Winton Brophy, who, along with her husband, Red, ran the Vista Verde Guest Ranch, within view of the Zirkel Wilderness. Winton's vegetables grew successfully in raised garden beds at an elevation of 7800 feet. She guided me through the seed companies that sold hardy cold-weather seeds and recommended the use of remay, a gauzy fabric to protect tender plants when it freezes, and the use of straw—not hay—for a good mulch.

Since then, for over forty years, I've put my hands in the soil in May, just like Dean. And the truth of the matter is my homesteading garden all those years ago didn't provide most of our food. Yes, we had lettuce, carrots, potatoes, onions, broccoli, and cabbage, but the weevils in the broccoli were hardier than I. The sauerkraut, shredded from my cabbage and proudly put up to ferment, grew mold. The sun shining on the Russets that eagerly peaked out above ground, produced a green toxin. When I asked Sam, a practical man, he laughed, "Well, I 'spose it will depend on how many of those potatoes you eat."

And again, this year, just like Dean, my garden failed to grow into the vision I had imagined in the spring. In late August, when I took my shovel out to harvest potatoes for dinner, I dug up more plants than usual to fill my strainer. Even though I've never had a crop quite like this—our country is perfect for potatoes—I assumed our very wet and cool June delayed some growth.

I planted my first rows of spinach and lettuce with optimism. I envisioned returning to the raised bed in a couple of weeks to plant successive rows, so we would have spinach and lettuce throughout the season. I never returned this summer to the lettuce bed. The yellow beans I planted as companion plants to the potatoes barely germinated. The entire summer's crop produced enough for three servings one night for dinner.

Beyond the borders of my raised vegetable beds, there was more to confess. In early June, when I tangled with errant meadow grasses along the western border of my largest perennial garden, I thought I'd won. I hadn't. While I was tempted to spray with one of the ranch's herbicides this year, I investigated natural barriers and put down a thick layer of newspapers (the ink today is environmentally safe) and an even thicker layer of cedar mulch. But the timothy and brome made its way back up through my environmentally conscious newspaper and cedar mulch barrier. I was simply defeated.

After failing to prune the raspberry patch, it invaded my

meditation garden, filled with ferns, bleeding hearts, and hostas, all in the shade of a small aspen grove. I never made time this summer to turn the wild growth back. Whenever I walked by the small Japanese stone tea house in the middle of my reflective garden, I was angry. I'd allowed the prickly interlopers to disturb the peace.

I confide I remain captured each spring by idealism in my gardening life, and I wonder if Dean doesn't too. Perhaps he planted in July, just like he does every year, knowing the season wouldn't be right if he didn't get his hands in the earth. He knew he'd miss the anticipation, those cool early mornings when all gardeners anxiously peek into the garden looking for the tiniest of miracles to emerge. He knew he'd miss walking out into the garden for an evening of harvesting a fresh crop of peas for supper.

Perhaps, too, in a landscape where the winter is long and deep, the planting ritual is an elixir, an antidote to too many dreary winter days carrying us away intoxicated like a bee after sucking its fill of nectar, blossom after blossom.

As we push the warm loam back and forth, our hands believe again in miracles. As we rest on the garden bench imagining the pea sprout and the frill of the first potato leaf, the sun's light rekindles our sleeping hearts and we take flight. And once we imbibe, we, like animals in the wild, know that we have returned to a familiar place.

I can't help but think Dean and I are both soothed by morning's light. With a simple handful of oddly sanguine seeds, we remember the surety we feel as we place each one in the soil. We see a new season through eyes that remember all the ones before, and the new and old bring renewal and peace. And it's then, in that moment, that I imagine Dean and I know that any further outcome in our gardens will pale, will fail to outshine the warmth and hope we feel as we dig up the earth and push a few dried-up seeds into the soil, no matter what day spring comes to our garden.

TWENTY-NINE

DENDRITES AND STARS

MAKE IT A PRACTICE TO WALK, HIKE, OR BIKE EVERY DAY. The habit is an old one. I grew up with forty-six other children on a subdivision block we called 21st Street. Most anytime I walked out the front door, I found friends eager to play. In the unencumbered time and space, my sense of self in relationship to the outside world settled in and with it a deep sense of well-being.

Now in my sixties, I can't wait to open the front door and head out. In good weather I often ride my bike along the North Fork of the Elk River in rural North Routt County. The paved road is called Seed House Road and passes by small, residential properties, often with horses in an adjoining pasture, or some part-time homes, like Grandma's Cabin tucked away in the pine and aspen near the river.

My ride begins easily into the shade of aspens where the air cools and sections of the North Fork of the Elk stretch out below the road. I eagerly follow its wind. As the road opens, the snow-capped divide on the horizon appears with sightings of Little Agnes and Big Agnes, Dome Peak, and the highest pinnacle, Mount Zirkel, at 12,180 feet, where summer may last six to eight weeks, depending upon the season.

There, at the headwaters of the North Fork, the wilderness consists of a diverse ecosystem from sagebrush meadows in the lower areas, through pine and spruce/fir forests, and on up to alpine tundra. Further on, where I eventually circle and turn around for my return ride home, the asphalt gives way to gravel, and those seeking hiking trails, fishing, and high mountain lakes drive further on to the Slavonia Trailhead to access the wilderness areas in the Park Range and Sierra Madre of the Continental Divide.

As I pedal, I'm always intrigued with the lap of the river, its speed and its flow. I contemplate the dynamic transformation of the waterway, from snow crystal to water droplet to roiling river in April, May, and June. I envision in the ambitious, headlong runoff, the geometrical elements once possessed by those crystals: needles, plates, and columns capped with dendrites and stars. High above in the deep snowpack, they now ease, relax, and let go of their organization and structure, becoming fluid, merging with all the other remnants of winter storms and silent nights.

I later learn the pace of the transformation is determined by overnight temperatures and the radiation from the sun. Heat converts the snow particles into water and gravity pulls the water to the ground. Then, over granite, roots, moss, and old soil, it flows to where resistance is least, into the shade and shadow of aspen-lined creeks like Hinman Creek, which joins Lester Creek, Colton Creek, and Willow Creek from the Hahn's Peak Basin to become the North Fork.

I pedal on, crossing Colton Creek and the guest ranch where an old gardening friend grew lettuce, rhubarb, and tomatoes at an elevation of 8000 feet. In another half-mile, it's Johnny Snyder's place, a small spot filled with an old square log home he built and chinked himself, the smoke from his woodstove often drifting up and away over the North Fork.

In 1960, Johnny came to the valley from Pennsylvania in a 1938 blue Pontiac pick-up. No one knows why. Described as a hard worker, a self-starter, he hired out first as a ranch hand and then as a woodsman, working the forests for logs and firewood. He, at one time, raised mink, the abandoned cages still intact near his house.

Late this past summer, Johnny carefully walked up the ramp to the local Clark Store. I've known him for forty years. That morning, I thought, surely, he's in his eighties. A friend told me he saw him that day too. Johnny told him, "I've got the cancer." A month later, neighbors found Johnny dead of a heart attack near the kitchen sink. Even though I had concluded that his reclusive heart had found a home embedded in the woods and the land, I was saddened by Johnny dying alone.

Where the pavement ends and the gravel begins, I loop around a small parking lot, stop, and unclip my shoes. To the east, I assess the melt on the divide, watching for the last of winter's remains; and back to the west, Sand Mountain stands near my point of return. A small meadow neighbors my resting spot, and in the still and quiet of the open land and high divide, I find a persistent peace.

In the respite, I, at times, consider the metamorphosis of those columns, plates, dendrites, and stars from crystalline form to water drop, roiling river, and back again to winter's crystals. I ask myself what similar transmutation do I understand as I stand bound to this earthly life. I can only relate to one transformation—from a spirit conceived, physically embodied, and born into the world. And then upon death, a complete change of form—the embodiment, the physical presence transformed back to spirit, just as crystalline forms melt to water drops and roiling river and back again to winter snows on the divide.

Recently, I recalled the time before my granddaughter was born, when she didn't exist in a physical form. Then I fast forward and she's wiggling in my arms and tracking me with her eyes, both her body and sweet spirit embedded in my life. Was her spirit traveling the world before it was captured to be here on earth in the natural world?

When I work at answering this question, I often think of my late mother. My kitchen window frames a view of the wilderness area near the North Fork. As I wash dishes, I imagine my mother's spirit sailing there on the wind and wonder if we will know one another again if I try sailing with her. I don't know. But I'll keep asking each time I ride along the North Fork, feeling the wash of the wave of the waterway just below Seed House Road.

Endnotes

1. Albert Schweitzer, *A Treasury of Albert Schweitzer*, (Philosophical Library/Open Road, 2014).

2. Boris Pasternak, "Some Statements," *The Poet's Work: 29 Poets on the Origins and Practice of Their Art,* ed. Reginald Gibbons (University of Chicago Press, 1989).

3. Parker J. Palmer, *On the Brink of Everything: Grace, Gravity and Getting Old* (Oakland, California: Berrett-Koehler Publishers, Inc., 2018).

4. Beth Kephart, "The Memoir in Pieces," *Creative Nonfiction*, 73 (Fall 2020) https://creativenonfiction.org/writing/the-memoir-in-pieces.

5. "Being and Time," Wikimedia Foundation (March 28, 2022) https://en.wikipedia.org/wiki/Being_and_Time.

6. Scott Russell Sanders, *Earth Works: Selected Essays* (Bloomington and Indianapolis: Indiana University Press, 2012).

7. Mark Nepo, *The Book of Awakening: Having the Life You Want by Being Present to the Life You Have* (Red Wheel Weiser, 2020).

8. Ralph Waldo Emerson, "Nature," American Transcendentalism Web, https://archive.vcu.edu/english/engweb/transcendentalism/authors/emerson/nature.html.

9. Terry Tempest Williams, *Refuge: An Unnatural History of Family and Place*. (New York: Vintage Books, A Division of Random House, 1991 and 2001).

10. Rory MacLean, "The Wilderness on Our Doorstep," *The Guardian* (August 2007) https://www.theguardian.com/travel/2007/aug/28/rorymaclean.travelbooks.

11. Sanders, *Earth Works.*

12. "Crisis Looms," *Climate Refugees,* http://www.climate-refugees.org.

13. Tom Di Liberto, "Cyclone Donna Churns in the South Pacific," *NOAA Climate* (May 10, 2017) https://www.climate.gov/news-features/event-tracker/cyclone-donna-churns-south-pacific.

14. Sanders, *Earth Works.*

15. Ernest Hemingway, *A Farewell to Arms,* (New York: Charles Scribner's Sons, 1938).

16. I've long forgotten the name of the person who said this.

17. James Hollis, *What Matters Most: Living a More Considered Life* (New York: Gotham Books, 2009).

18. Eldon Greij, "Bird Basics: Six Different Feather Types Explained," *Bird Watching Online* (March 31, 2016) https://www.birdwatchingdaily.com/news/science/bird-basics-six-different-feather-types-explained.

19. Parker J. Palmer, *On the Brink of Everything.*

20 "Erik Erikson's Stages of Psychosocial Development," last updated July 28, 2021, https://www.verywellmind.com/erik-eriksons-stages-of-psychosocial-development-2795740.

21. Christopher Moreman, "On the Relationship Between Birds and Spirits of the Dead," *Society & Animals Journal* (2014), 1–22.

22. Moreman.

23. Jean Amery, *On Aging: Revolt and Resignation* (Bloomington and Indianapolis: Indiana University Press, 1994).

24. Ruth Garfield, "Facing Death: Intrapsychic Conflict and Intergenerational Passage," *The Wound Mortality: Fear, Denial, and Acceptance of Death,* ed. Salman Akhtar (New York: Jason Aronson, 2010).

25. Chris Arthur, "Of Solitude," *After Montaigne: Contemporary Essayists Cover the Essays,* ed. David Lazar and Patrick Madden (Athens, Georgia: The University of Georgia Press, 2015).

26. Muriel Strode, *A Soul's Faring* (New York: Boni and Liveright, 1921)

OTHER SOURCES

Armstrong, Karen. *The Case for God*. New York: Anchor Books, Division of Random House, 2009.

Blew, Mary Clearman. *Bone Deep in Landscape: Writing, Reading, and Place*. Norman, Oklahoma: University of Oklahoma Press, 1999.

Carlson, Laurie Winn. *Cattle: An Informal Social History*. Chicago, Illinois: Ivan R. Dee, 2001.

deBuys, William. *The Walk*. San Antonio, Texas: Trinity University Press, 2007.

Elson, Louis C. *Elson's Pocket Music Dictionary*. Bryn Mawr, Pennsylvania: Oliver Ditson Company, 1909.

Fletcher, Harrison Candelaria. *Descanso for My Father: Fragments of Life*. Lincoln, Nebraska: University of Nebraska Press, 2012.

Frank, Steve. "New government report reveals staggering economic and health toll of climate change." *CBS News Online*. November 23, 2018. https://www.cbsnews.com/news/climate-change-report-national-climate-assessment-released-today-reveals-economic-health-toll-climate-change-2018-11-23.

Frost, Robert. "Mending Wall." *Poetry Foundation*. https://www.poetryfoundation.org/poems/44266/mending-wall.

Gonzales, Laurence. *Deep Survival: Who Lives, Who Dies, and Why*. New York and London: W. W. Norton and Company, 2003.

Katie, Byron with Stephen Mitchell. *Loving What Is: Four Questions That Can Change Your Life*. New York: Harmony Books, 2002.

Lopez, Barry and Debra Gwartney. *Home Ground: Language for an American Landscape*. San Antonio, Texas: Trinity University Press, 2006.

McKee, Robert. *Story: Substance, Structure, Style, and the Principles of Screenwriting*. London: Methuen Publishing Limited, 1999.

Mann, Michael. "Dr. Michael Mann on Extreme Weather: 'We Predicted This Long Ago.'" *The Climate Reality Project*. October 21, 2017. https://www.climaterealityproject.org/blog/dr-michael-mann-extreme-weather-we-predicted-long-ago.

Oliver, Mary. *Evidence: Poems*. Boston: Beacon Press, 2009.

Oliver, Mary. *Upstream: Selected Essays*. New York: Penguin Press, 2016.

Pyne, Steve. "Moved by Fire: History's Promethean Moment." *The Appendix: In Motion* 2, no. 4 (October 2014). http://theappendix.net/issues/2014/10/moved-by-fire-historys-promethean-moment.

Sanders, Scott Russell. *The Force of Spirit*. Beacon Press, 2001.

"Special Correspondence from Long Gulch." *Steamboat Pilot* (October 25, 1916). https://www.coloradohistoricnewspapers.org/cgi- bin/colorado?a=d&d=STP19161025&e=--- ----en-20--1--txt-txIN--------0-.

"Special Correspondence from Long Gulch." *Steamboat Pilot* (July 2, 1919). https://www.coloradohistoricnewspapers.org/cgi-bin/colorado?a=d&d=STP19190702&e=---- ---en-20--1--txt-txIN--------0-.

Temperton, James. "Why it's time we all became climate change optimists." *Wired* 26 (November 2018). https://www.wired.co.uk/article/climate-change-optimism-paris-agreement.

"The Will to Change." *Cool It: Climate Change Issue National Geographic* (November 2015).

Walker, Nicole. "Of Constancy." *After Montaigne: Contemporary Essayists Cover the Essays*. Edited by David Lazar and Patrick Madden. Athens, Georgia: The University of Georgia Press, 2015.

About the Author

Mary B. Kurtz's work has appeared in *Amsterdam Quarterly, The Hong Kong Review, Ruminate Magazine, Braided Way, The Colorado Sun, BlueHouse Journal, Writers Workshop Review,* and *Speckled Trout Review.* Her first collection of essays, *At Home in the Elk River Valley: Reflections on Family, Place, and the West,* was recognized as a 2012 Regional Nonfiction Finalist by the National Indie Excellence Book Award program. It was also the recipient of the Colorado Independent Publishers Association's 2012 Bronze EVVY Award. Kurtz received her MFA in creative writing from Regis University. She and her husband raise quarter horses, cattle, and hay on their ranch in the Elk River Valley of northwestern Colorado.

—www.marybkurtz.com

SHANTI ARTS

NATURE ▪ ART ▪ SPIRIT

Please visit us online
to browse our entire book catalog,
including poetry collections and fiction,
books on travel, nature, healing, art,
photography, and more.

Also take a look at our highly regarded art
and literary journal, *Still Point Arts Quarterly*,
which may be downloaded for free.

www.shantiarts.com

CPSIA information can be obtained
at www.ICGtesting.com
Printed in the USA
BVHW030921240922
647878BV00008B/30